The Wisdom of Solitude

三十棒

The Wisdom of Solitude

A Zen Retreat in the Woods

Jane Dobisz

HarperSanFrancisco

A Division of HarperCollins*Publishers*

Calligraphy from *The Whole World Is a Single Flower*, Zen Master Seung Sahn. Published by Charles E. Tuttle Co., Inc., of Boston, MA, and Tokyo, Japan.

THE WISDOM OF SOLITUDE: *A Zen Retreat in the Woods.* Copyright © 2004 by Jane Dobisz. All rights reserved. Printed in the United States of America. No part of this book may be used or reproduced in any manner whatsoever without written permission except in the case of brief quotations embodied in critical articles and reviews. For information address HarperCollins Publishers, Inc., 10 East 53rd Street, New York, NY 10022.

HarperCollins books may be purchased for educational, business, or sales promotional use. For information please write: Special Markets Department, HarperCollins Publishers, Inc., 10 East 53rd Street, New York, NY 10022.

HarperCollins Web site: http://www.harpercollins.com

HarperCollins®, ▨®, and HarperSanFrancisco™ are trademarks of HarperCollins Publishers, Inc.

Book design by Ralph L. Fowler

FIRST EDITION

Library of Congress Cataloging-in-Publication Data is available upon request.

ISBN 0–06–008595–9

03 04 05 06 07 ❖RRD(H) 10 9 8 7 6 5 4 3 2 1

For my teacher,

Zen Master Seung Sahn,

and my daughter,

Olivia Rose

The Human Route

Coming empty-handed, going empty-handed, that is human.
When you are born, where do you come from?
When you die, where do you go?
Life is like a floating cloud, which appears.
Death is like a floating cloud, which disappears.
The floating cloud itself originally does not exist.
Life and death, coming and going, are also like that.
But there is one thing that always remains clear.
It is pure and clear,
Not depending on life and death.

Then what is the one pure and clear thing?

—Traditional Chinese Poem

Contents

Hard Training

Spring Comes

Introduction

All the great Zen teachings say that the wisdom of the universe is right in front of us. They say that, deep down inside, each of us knows we are complete. The question is, How do we make that truth come alive in our own experience of life?

At a fairly young age, it struck me that this was a very important point—and that if I could somehow get to it, the secret of happiness was in my own heart. I'd always heard that the great sages were in Asia, and decided on Nepal as a logical place to begin. Not long after that, I found myself stepping off an Air-India plane onto the tarmac at the Kathmandu airport. It was dark outside. The air felt different on my skin, not at all like the air in the West. It smelled exotic, full of diesel and spice and earth. "This was the right choice, to come here," I thought to myself. I was stepping on Eastern ground into a new life.

I stayed with a wonderful Nepalese family on the outskirts of Kathmandu, enrolled in a school for foreigners, and made inquiries about meeting Buddhist teachers. I'm embarrassed to admit that for the first few weeks in Nepal I didn't see the Himalayas at all. Focused exclusively on the foothills, I kept thinking to myself, "What's all the fuss? These look rather like the mountains we have back home in Vermont." Then one day, while walking home after school, I looked high up in the sky and realized for the first time that those white things way up there that I had previously thought were *clouds* were actually the snow-covered peaks of the mountains themselves!

That's how high they are!

I had one of those "Aha!" moments as I stared up at them, stupefied. So these were the mountains the wise masters lived in! And these would be what I would have to climb if I wanted to meet them. How would I, of zero climbing experience, ever make it up there?

Though somewhat intimidated, after a few months of researching where to go I was finally ready to make the journey. I headed off with two new friends on the Pokhara-Jomosom route, as it did not require serious mountaineering experience and equipment. Even so, it was more than strenuous enough for our little team, who had never climbed anything bigger than your average hill.

The grandeur and magnificence of the Himalayan mountain range is unimaginable. There are peaks in every direction, jagged, snowy, benevolent, and menacing all at once. We saw things you never see in Rhode Island, where I am from: small tribes of exotic looking people walking by with bureaus on their heads, wearing glass bracelets and silver nose rings. A wandering ascetic, his white hair in a tangle of dreadlocks, with a live snake curling around his staff, smiling at us half-crazy and half-toothless. A crystal-clear Himalayan pool filled with sari-clad women, splashing around with their bare-shouldered kids, toothy grins everywhere. A forest of rhododendron trees in full bloom. Being in a country where these were everyday occurrences woke up every dormant sense of adventure and mystery I never knew I had. Ironically, in this setting I really didn't care anymore what the meaning of life was. It was enough to just be there. But underneath the novelty of it, I knew the big questions I had come with would remain unresolved until I dealt with them somehow. After all, I reasoned with myself, I wouldn't always be on this trek, captivated by majestic scenes out of an IMAX movie.

We climbed and we rested, meeting people of every nationality along the way. My friends Sue and Laurie and I had a great time together. Whether we were chowing down pumpkin soup and the traditional *dal bhat* (rice and lentils) at the end of a long day's climb or laughing at night in our tent, we were happy. One night, we were invited to sleep over with a Nepalese family we had met on the way. When we got to their house, we were surprised to find it was made out of nothing but dried leaves and sticks. While we were waiting for our dinner of three boiled potatoes each, the father of the house went out in search of food with his bow and arrow. No minivan, no drive-through, and nary an ATM machine in sight. Not only did I feel I had traveled to the other side of the world geographically speaking, I also felt as though I'd gone back in time to a place that existed only in history books. It was fundamentally mind-altering to be there, and we were relishing every minute of it.

Two weeks into the trek there it was! The small temple I had been looking for! Inside that ancient tile-roofed structure was the all-knowing one who would answer the great questions of life and death for me. At last, I was to meet a real live Tibetan lama. Heart pounding, I knocked at the gate, certain that when the lama saw me, he'd immediately recognize I wasn't enlightened and shout, "Go away, you parasite!"

A beautiful Tibetan woman answered the door.

"Is the lama in?"

She smiled a brilliant white, ultrabright smile and said, "Lama? Not here! Lama, New York."

"The lama is in New York?" I asked incredulously.

"Yes, yes, New York! You come back again!"

I sat down on a big rock and laughed out loud. Always the long way! I could have taken a four-hour train ride to New York, and here I was, unemployed, without a home to return to, on the side of a Himalayan mountain. Looking out over the vast rhododendron forest at the glorious snow-covered peaks in the distance, I realized that everything I was seeking was a lot closer to home than I'd previously imagined. So close in fact, I was staring at it.

Being a great believer in perseverance, I kept knocking on other temple doors until I thankfully found some lamas who were in. Like loving grandfathers, they generously gave their time and helped me get started on the path of practicing meditation.

It ultimately ended up being a good thing that the first lama was in New York. As luck would have it, many spiritual masters from Asia had settled in the United States to teach us

Western barbarians. After coming home from Nepal, I discovered a large network of teachers from Asia right here in the States. Taking advantage of the opportunity to learn from them, I attended many Buddhist retreats over the next few years. One year, at the end of a ninety-day meditation retreat in Barre, Massachusetts, two guests were invited to speak to our group of about a hundred students. One was Zen Master Seung Sahn (also called "Dae Soen Sa Nim"), and the other was one of his senior students, Zen Master Su Bong. They were quite a presence, the two of them, with their bright eyes, hearty laughs, and cryptic responses to questions from the audience.

Whenever anyone asked Zen Master Seung Sahn a question, he picked up his Zen stick and said, "I hit you thirty times!"

Finally, I raised my hand and asked him, "You keep saying, 'I hit you thirty times!' Do you really hit people?"

"Come up here!" he commanded, feigning the tough-guy imperial Zen master, though the twinkle in his eye gave him away. He was having fun, and so were we.

I approached the front of the meditation hall where he was seated cross-legged on the floor.

"Sit here." He motioned for me to sit down on the floor in front of him. Then, clapping his hands together, he said, "Take this sound, and bring it here!"

Without thinking I gave him a big high-five, slapping his hand in the air. He laughed loudly and said, "Wonderful, wonderful! That's Zen mind."

It was unlike any conversation I'd ever had, and I liked it very much. In that moment I recognized this man as my teacher.

Zen Master Seung Sahn is a widely revered Zen patriarch from Korea. He's got an infectious laugh and a mind that can meet anyone, regardless of the situation. His teaching is streamlined to the point of brilliance. Even after all these years as his student, I haven't grasped one-tenth of all he has to impart. Of course that makes it all the more interesting to study with him. When he was a young man growing up under the Japanese occupation in Korea, his overwhelming passion had been to liberate his country. He became involved in the underground Korean independence movement and was briefly imprisoned for transmitting information to resistance leaders in Shanghai and Manchuria. He narrowly escaped a death sentence when a high-ranking official pulled the strings for his release.

Still in his early twenties, tired of politics and disillusioned with society, he cut his hair and went into the mountains alone to do an arduous retreat for one hundred days. From that point until the present day he has lived as a Buddhist monk and actively taught people all over the world how to practice Zen.

Here was a man whose direction in life was the clearest I'd ever seen. What happened to him on that hundred-day retreat? Why not try it? The whole idea of being alone had always intrigued me, yet at the same time scared me half to death. Being alone would mean no human contact, no talking, no going to work, paying bills, running errands, or doing any of the usual things I spent so much energy on. What would that be like? Who would I find there, underneath all the layers of social conditioning, obligations, rules, and cultural filters? What was the raw material made of? Would I even like this person? Would she be someone wonderful or horrible? Would she be strong or weak? Deep or shallow? Or all of those things combined? It seemed the best way to find out would be to follow the traditional monastic schedule of sitting, walking, chanting, bowing, and cutting wood for one hundred days. During all these activities in every moment I would repeat the Great Dharani mantra (the text of which is in the Appendix), as Dae Soen Sa Nim had done.

In one way, it doesn't make sense that one could engage in such simple activity all day and find deep wisdom in it, yet this is exactly what the ancients figured out a long time ago and have been trying to tell us about ever since. A wonderful story illustrating this point involves a Sufi master named Mullah Nasrudin. One day, his student went to visit him. He happened to sneak up from behind, intending to surprise Mullah, when he noticed that he was sprinkling bread crumbs around the perimeter of the garden.

"Mullah, what on earth are you doing?"

"Oh, this? It's my technique for keeping the tigers away."

"But Mullah," the student replied, "there are no tigers for miles around here!"

"Effective, isn't it?" said Mullah.

As with Mullah Nasrudin's bread crumbs, as unusual as they may seem, the techniques of bowing, sitting, chanting, walking, working, and eating meditation used on traditional Zen retreats are indeed effective. As for me, I knew there were still plenty of tigers stalking around in my mind:

"What am I?"

"What is life?"

"What is death?"

It was time to set them free.

Since I had already been to the Himalayas and back again, it occurred to me that I didn't have to be in an exotic locale like Tibet or Korea for such an undertaking. I made plans to do a one-hundred-day solo Zen retreat in the woods of New England, with no idea of what would happen or even if I would make it through the first week. At a bare minimum, I would find out the limitations of my mind. If what the Zen books said was true, maybe there are no limitations. An old Zen teaching puts it this way: "If your mind is complete, the sun, the moon, the stars . . . everything is complete. If your mind is not complete, then the sun, moon, and stars are not enough. You will feel as though there is something missing."

Most of us don't have the opportunity or the desire to go off alone for such a long time, but we desperately need to rest our minds in this busy world we live in. As Dae Soen Sa Nim always says, how you keep your mind in this moment is more important than any kind of specific technique. You don't have to be a wandering ascetic, hermit, monk, or nun to experience spiritual depth in your own everyday life. If you stop and take a few moments of silence and solitude each day, you can build wisdom into your life that will emanate into the way you think, feel, and act.

If your mind is clear in this moment, your whole life is clear.

If your life is clear, this world is a better place.

Arriving

1   Where Are You Going?

Buddha is your mind
And the Way goes nowhere.
Don't look for anything but this.
If you point your cart north
When you want to go south,
How will you arrive?

—Zen Master Ryokan

HE TINY CABIN is in a small clearing in the middle of the woods. The ground is covered in a foot of snow. It's the middle of January. Two friends help me unload enough provisions to last the winter, see to it that I get somewhat settled in, then drive away just at twilight. "Bye! See you in May! Have a great retreat!"

The rock song on the car radio recedes into the distance as they drive away down the three-mile dirt road that leads toward "civilization." It's getting darker. The wind is picking up. My stomach feels empty. To make a cup of tea I have to first boil water. To boil water I have to build a fire from scratch. What was I thinking, doing this?

I have fifty pounds of rice, ten pounds of red adzuki beans, five pounds of soybeans, ten pounds of sunflower seeds, four containers of miso, one lunch bag of dried fruit, two large bags of roasted barley tea, and a medium-sized jar of Skippy peanut butter. This is my food supply for the next one hundred days. I won't be going out of the woods to town until the spring. No one will be visiting me.

What if something happens and I need help? What if some lunatic finds out I'm alone up here with no lock on the door?

In my desire to emulate the ancients, I foolishly decided not to bring coffee either, let alone cream or sugar.

This is not what you'd call cozy.

The wooden cabin is L-shaped, about 150 square feet total. There's nothing in it but a cast-iron wood-burning stove, a twin bed, a built-in set of shelves, one green wooden chair, and an old end table. Pine floors and pine walls. The sink isn't hooked up to any plumbing, which seems kind of odd. I wonder why it's there at all, and then realize it's really just a big ceramic basin with a hole in it. A white plastic bucket sits underneath the drain. Outside on the porch there's some stacked wood, an enamel chamber pot, a five-gallon red plastic jug, a few tools, and an ax. For water, there's a well down the path, about a quarter mile away.

I post the schedule on the wall with a thumbtack:

3:15 A.M. . . . . Wake Up

3:20 . . . . 300 Bows

4:00 . . . . Tea

4:15 . . . . Sitting

4:45 . . . . Walking

4:55 . . . . Sitting

5:30 . . . . Walking

5:40 . . . . Sitting

6:10 . . . . Walking

6:20 . . . . Sitting

6:50 . . . . Chanting

7:40 . . . . Breakfast

8:00 . . . . Work Period

9:30 . . . . Break

10:00 . . . . 300 Bows

10:30 . . . . Tea

10:40 . . . . Sitting

11:10 . . . . Walking

11:20 . . . . Sitting

11:50 . . . . Walking

12:00 P.M. . . . . Lunch

12:20 . . . . Break

1:00 . . . . 200 Bows

1:30 . . . . Sitting

2:00 . . . . Walking

2:20 . . . . Sitting

2:50 . . . . Walking

3:00 . . . . Sitting

3:30 . . . . Walking

3:40 . . . . Sitting

4:10 . . . . Long Walk

5:15	Tea Break
6:00	200 Bows
6:30	Chanting
7:30	Sitting
8:00	Walking
8:10	Sitting
8:40	Walking
8:50	Sitting
9:20	Last Two Chants
9:30	Sleep

The retreat schedule is the core framework of the Zen experience. There's time for sitting, walking, chanting, work, eating, and rest, all in balance. I officially begin following it tomorrow morning at 3:15. My eyes linger for a moment on its military-like format. Will I be able to adhere to the ridiculously early wake-up and all the hours of sitting and bowing with no one here to check up on me?

I finish unpacking. There aren't many clothes to put away, just some long underwear, sweatpants, work clothes, and boots. I stack them neatly on the shelf by the bed and place a wooden Buddha on the table with two candles, an incense burner, and a water bowl. I double-check the batteries in the flashlight and in the alarm clock, and take a few deep breaths as the full weight of the silence and my utter aloneness settles over me. I am happy and scared, both sure and unsure at the same time.

As I crawled into the sleeping bag that first night, my last thought was, "One down, ninety-nine to go." I hoped the fire's sparks wouldn't fly out and ignite a blaze that would turn the whole cabin into a ball of flames, killing me before I even got started. I lay there wondering whether, as a preventive measure, I should get up and put the fire out with a bucket of water.

How would I get it started the next morning if the ashes were all wet?

What did the Native Americans do in their teepees before the days of electric heat? How did they keep the children warm at night if the fires were put out? On the other hand, if they left fires burning, wouldn't sparks fly out, land on their blankets, and burn them all to death?

These were the deep thoughts I had my first night in the woods. I was raised in the suburbs and don't know much about the details of chopping wood and building fires. I guess I'm going to learn. It's lonely the first night.

Very lonely.

Thank God I'm too young to know any better. I'm too resilient and curious and excited. One should do all these things in one's youth. As you get older, it's easy to find reasons to stay comfortable.

2 The Alarm

we're lost born in delusions deeper than any mind
if you could escape awakening you'd ripen like a pear all by itself

—Zen Master Ikkyu, *Crow with No Mouth*

N O W O N D E R they call it an "alarm"! Adrenaline floods through my veins at the sound of the alarm clock on the first morning. The fire evidently went out by itself after all. At least the cabin didn't burn down. Still in the sleeping bag, clutching a *mala* (a string of beads) in my right hand, I make a stab at doing the mantra I'm supposed to be doing at all times: *Shim yo jung gu dae dharani*, it begins. It is immediately interrupted with thoughts of "Where am I?" "Where's the flashlight?" "I can't see anything," and other such matters.

Unable to get up, I'm paralyzed by a powerful train of thought that tells me that it's the first day, after all, and no one is here, after all, and I should probably rest up a little and start at 9:00 A.M. Yes, that would be a good idea. I could get off to a much better start and that way, fully oriented to my new surroundings, I could start following the early-morning schedule *tomorrow*.

An aerial snapshot from the roof of the cabin at that moment would have shown only a puffy blue sleeping bag. If you looked closer, though, you would have noticed a red, frozen nose and two panicked eyes staring out of the top of the bag, as if to say, "What in the world am I doing here??!!"

In the inky darkness, I can't see anything. A voice in my head yells at me, "Get up, you lazy dog! If you sleep in on the very first morning, you're completely worthless!" Unzipping the cozy womb of the bag, I swing a leg onto the cold, hard pine boards of the floor. Still unfamiliar with the layout of the cabin, I grope my way around, crashing into sharp objects until feeling the cold iron surface of the woodstove. Eventually I find the matches. Teeth chattering, hands shaking, I light one after another, holding them aloft like little torches until I can locate a candle. I find the kerosene lanterns and light them too. The next step is unquestionably to make a fire.

I already forgot from last night, do I turn all these little levers on the stove to the left or to the right? I crinkle up newspaper as fast as my hands allow, then layer on the kindling. Smoke pours back into the cabin, into my eyes and throat. I fiddle with the levers until the smoke goes up the chimney instead of into my face. Crouching in front of the stove's open door, I bask a while in the dry crackling warmth of the flames and feed in a few thin logs once the fire catches.

I'm starting to wake up.

I can do this.

As if by magic the mantra kicks in again. *Namak alya baro gije sebaraya, moji sadabaya, maha sadabaya* . . .

If I start thinking too much about the fact that I'm going to be alone for the next hundred days, waking up to mornings like this, I'll no doubt pack my bags and go home right now. If I stop to wonder why I should *bow* in the middle of a bunch of trees, or whose idea was this anyway, I will never proceed.

Zen is not about why the forms are this way or that way, who invented them, what their cultural significance is, or any of that—though it makes a fine syllabus in an academic religion class. The practice of Zen (as opposed to the study of Zen) is something altogether different: to give yourself completely to each moment as it is—whether it is doing a mantra, stumbling in the dark, or feeling the fire's warm heat on your skin. It requires a complete suspension of disbelief, which amounts to trusting that there is something much deeper than reason and logic, and that if you follow it, you might just end up where you belong.

No analyzing.

It's time to start bowing.

Just do it.

3 Up and Down

*"Zen Master, why do we do all these bows? Who are we
bowing to?"*

*"You are not bowing to anyone outside. When you bow,
it's your small self bowing to your true self—that's all."*

—Zen Master Seung Sahn

Up. Down.
Up. Down.
Up. Down.

Barely awake, I tell myself to "just do it" while stealing a
quick glance back at the bed. The sleeping bag looks so in-
viting. Thoughts run through my head about why it would be
better to bow after it gets light out. Normally an expert procras-
tinator, susceptible to excuses of any sort, even I can't get away
with rationalizing in this case. At 3:20 in the morning, alone in
the middle of the woods, it's not like there's anywhere else I
have to be. I continue with the bows.

Up. Down.

Up. Down.

Up. Down.

Three hundred times. Each time a bow has been completed, I move one bead on the mala to keep count while repeating the mantra in my mind. The rhythm of the movement and the sound of the mantra working in tandem cut through all the foggy thinking and wake me up.

Here in the West we don't bow to anything or anyone. Not to God, not to Buddha, not to our parents, not to each other. It would never occur to us to bow because this is a democracy and we are all equal. In the East however, everyone is always bowing to everyone else. It is a sign of respect, a greeting, a religious practice, and simply a chance to pause.

Bowing is the act of our small self bowing to our true self. Our small self is the "I, my, me" that feels like a separate person. It's the one who thinks "I'm Jane, I'm a mother" or "I am Bob, I'm a doctor." Our true self has no idea of being separate because it is before all ideas and thinking. Like the way water always flows to the sea or a tree grows up, up, up, our true self just does its job, without the added burden of thinking about it. When we bow, we aren't bowing to anything outside of our own true nature. Each bow is a chance to wake up from the illusion that we are somehow separate from the universe. In the physicality of palms touching the mat, of knees on the ground, and of standing up again, there is only the activity of bowing.

Zen Master Seung Sahn, in his inimitable English, says bowing is the "number one quick way to make your karma disappear." Sometimes I think he decided to take bows to a whole new level as he launched his brand of Zen in the West. For twenty or more years he has done a thousand bows a day, no matter what. Sick, tired, traveling, on trains, in hotel rooms . . . he never misses them. Just watching him do that day in and day out has itself been a big teaching.

And here I am, young and strong. After only three hundred bows my legs are shaking like two jelly gummi worms. The schedule is proving to be a formidable master, and it's only the first activity of the first day.

Thirsty now.

A cup of tea would be good.

4   Three Pounds of Flax

*Once, Zen Master Dong Sahn was in the market, weighing
out some flax.*
  A monk asked him, "What is Buddha?"
  Without hesitation he replied, "Three pounds of flax."

—*Mu Mun Kwan*

POUR A CUP OF TEA from the cast-iron kettle. Though
its roasted barley flavor is robust, I lament that it isn't coffee, light with one sugar. Looking around at the dimly lit
walls, I can't quite tell if this feels cozy, here in the predawn
blackness, or if it feels deathlike. Ever the optimist, I choose
the "cozy" view and settle in for the first sitting session of the
morning. I start to repeat the mantra quietly, and my mind
wanders.

I return to the mantra.

My mind wanders again.

I come back.

It sounds incredibly stupid, doesn't it? That a person should have to try so hard to simply be where she already is, yet this is my predicament.

The first time I tried sitting meditation was in a class of about twenty people. We were instructed to kill our "I." Rather than accomplishing this mean feat, I nearly killed everyone around me instead. The head teacher, in charge of signaling the end of the sitting, sat cross-legged at the front of the room with a saintly expression on his face. Convinced he had lost track of the time, I had all I could do to keep from screaming out, "Ring the bell, you idiot!!" Judging from their placid expressions, I could only assume that those around me had reached the state of nirvana, but I only sat there wondering, Where is the bliss in the pain in my knees and in the screaming boredom of sitting unmoving? What's so great about encountering all those vulnerable parts of myself I don't want to meet anyway? This was not at all like the image I'd had in my head of being seated cross-legged on the floor blissfully communing with the universe.

I couldn't wait to get out of there.

This is the irony of spiritual practice. We travel far and wide, scraping and clawing our way to some meditation center, temple, or mountain cabin; enthusiastically enroll in a meditation class, and then, once there, pray for it to end as quickly as possible so we can go home and relax. When the class is over, we hurry home to our comfort zone, where we can safely wish to be practicing again. No matter where we are, we are always wishing we were somewhere else. What we continually forget is that we can only be where we are in any given moment. Our mad dash toward God knows what perpetuates this feeling of always being somewhat removed from our actual lives.

One of the most helpful analogies for what sitting meditation is like comes from a great teacher in the Vipassana tradition named Joseph Goldstein. Joseph compares meditation practice with training a puppy to stay. The puppy is our thinking mind. It runs here, scampers there, wagging its tail and sniffing things, and in general acts according to its nature. Meditation is the practice of bringing the puppy back as we say, "Stay."

For example, say your meditation practice is counting the breaths. You start out, "One, two, . . ." and then, before you know it, the puppy has gone to Los Angeles, or to yesterday's football game, or to a list of things you must accomplish. Rather than follow the puppy randomly here and there, you pick it up and gently bring it back to the breath: "One . . . two . . . three. . . ." Over time, the puppy learns to stay with you. Not that there is anything wrong with the puppy's nature—it's just that after chasing after it day in and day out, what do you really end up with?

This staying power is the foundation of all the different meditation techniques. Some people count their breaths or follow the sensation of the breath. Some visualize a picture or image. Others repeat a phrase over and over quietly in their minds, which is called a mantra. It doesn't matter which technique you use. The one thing they all have in common is this: they do not require thinking. As the Confucian scholar Lao-tzu once said, "Thinking only goes as far as that which it can understand."

Zen asks, "Then what?"

That's the ten thousand dollar question.

5 The Great Way Has No Gate

"The Great Way has no gate."
How do you pass through?

—Zen Master Seung Sahn

THE BEST WAY to boil water quickly is to put it in a pot on the stove, turn the flame up to high, and leave it there until the water boils. If you keep taking the pot off the flame, letting it cool down, and then putting it back on the burner, the water will never boil. In the same way, the idea in retreat practice is to turn up the flame of awareness during sitting and then leave it on "high" during all the other activities of the day, including walking, bowing, eating, and working. There are no breaks. Everything is part of the practice.

It's now time for walking meditation, which has no destination or goal other than paying attention to every step. Standing up from the cushion, I walk slowly back and forth across the cabin, letting my mind sink down into the soles of my feet on the warm pinewood floor, continuing to repeat the mantra. The cabin is pretty small, so every ten steps or so I turn around and go back the other way.

Back and forth for ten minutes.

This is walking meditation.

It's difficult not to be "on the way" somewhere while walking. Many meditation teachers say that during walking meditation you should take every step as though it were your first—or your last. That way you will appreciate each step. It's these small moments we take for granted, but these small moments are actually so important. They are the units that compose our life. Zen practice helps us to discover that everything we ever wanted is right here in front of us, if only we can slow down and recognize it.

My eighty-two-year-old neighbor named Herb has mastered this. He recently spent thirteen weeks in the hospital, during which time he underwent two major surgeries and nearly died. At one point he was so weak he couldn't even sit up, let alone get out of his bed and walk. As he slowly recovered, he regained enough strength in his legs to stand. One day when I went in to visit him, he looked up from his bed, eyes shining with joy, and proclaimed, "I walked today! Two hundred and forty steps!"

"Keep a mind like that during walking meditation," I tell myself. Do the mantra. Put one foot in front of the other and go. Pass through the "Great Way that has no gate."

Then what?

See the sky, only blue.

See the trees, only green.

6 Wooden Fish

after all your talk of food . . . you're still hungry
after all your talk of clothes . . . you're still cold
eating rice is what fills your belly
wearing clothes is what keeps you warm
without really thinking it through
you grumble that the way to find Buddha is difficult
look inside your heart . . . there's Buddha
don't look for him outside your self

—Zen poet Han Shan, *The View from Cold Mountain*

BEFORE CHANTING I light the candles and a stick of incense, bow to the Buddha, and pick up a wooden instrument called a *moktak*. The moktak is shaped like a round fish head with a slit in it. When you bang on the fish's head, it makes a hollow *tok tok tok* sound.

A typical line in one of the chants goes like this: *jung-gu-op-jin-on-su-ri-su-ri-ma-ha-su-ri-su-su-ri-sa-ba-ha*. The melody is ancient and hauntingly beautiful. During chanting, when my mind wanders off to think about this or that, I bring it back to the sound of the syllable I'm on. SU. JIN. OP. With all energy and attention focused on each syllable, there's no room for thinking to wiggle in. Like everything else in Zen, chanting is yet one more way to pay attention in this moment.

Chanting practice uses sound as a means to us wake up. Perceiving sound in its purest sense means listening without preconceived ideas of any kind. When we perceive the sound of someone's voice, without adding our opinions and judgments, we can hear what that person is really trying to say, rather than running his or her words through the filter of whether or not we agree with that point of view, and so on.

Dae Soen Sa Nim's teacher was a Zen monk in Korea named Zen Master Ko Bong. One winter, Ko Bong stayed in the mountain temple of a scholarly monk who performed Buddhist ceremonies for the people in that area. One day when the scholarly monk was out, a woman knocked on the temple door. Ko Bong opened it.

"Oh, wonderful! You are here! Today is the memorial day of one of our members. We need a monk to come and perform a ceremony for him this afternoon. Can you do it, sir?"

As a Zen monk, Ko Bong had no knowledge of ceremonial matters, but, hearing her sincere request, he said to the woman, "Of course." She escorted him to a nearby mountain temple. Though unfamiliar with the traditional memorial chanting ceremony, Ko Bong lit a stick of incense, picked up the moktak, and began. He patched together chants he remembered from here and there, adding on a few stray Buddhist sutras for good measure. He chanted for quite some time, bowed to the altar, and bid the woman farewell. She thanked him profusely, pleased to have honored her friend on the anniversary of his death. Later that afternoon she bumped into the scholarly monk returning home on the mountain road.

"Hello, Sunim (venerable monk)! Ko Bong was at our temple today. He conducted a wonderful memorial ceremony. Everyone was very happy."

"How can that be? Ko Bong doesn't know any of the ceremonial chanting."

As it turned out, the woman was a retired nun and had known all along that Ko Bong had been improvising.

"I know," she replied, "but it didn't matter, it was still the most wonderful ceremony. Technically, Ko Bong didn't know the right words, but he hit the moktak and chanted his heart out anyway, just to help us. This is what true chanting is all about."

There are many legends about the power of chanting in the Buddhist tradition. One famous story is about the origin of the moktak itself. A long time ago in China, a government official and his young family were enjoying a boating trip on a gorgeous lake. Unbeknownst to them, their little baby fell overboard into the deep water. When her family discovered she was missing, they and several local fishermen searched the waters all day and night to save her, but unfortunately they did not find her anywhere. The grief-stricken parents then went to a monk named Chung San Poep Sa and asked him to perform a funeral ceremony for their daughter. "We can't even find her body to give her a proper funeral!" the mother sobbed.

Chung San Poep Sa went into deep meditation and immediately perceived exactly where this little girl was. He told them to go to the fish market right away and search for the largest fish on the heap. Puzzled, they followed Chung San's advice. When they bought the fish and cut it open, there was their daughter, inside the fish's belly—alive and well! From that day forward, the whole family felt such gratitude toward all sea creatures they never ate fish again. This is why the moktak is shaped like a fish with an open mouth and empty stomach. The meaning is, "The baby is still alive." When we chant, we can save all beings. We can find the lost baby.

I pick up the moktak and chant. *Namak alya baro gije sebaraya, moji sadabaya, maha sadabaya . . .*

It's clear.

All language is one language.

All sound is one sound.

7 Go Wash Your Bowls

A monk asked Joju, "I have just entered the monastery. Please,
teach me, Master."
   Joju said, "Have you had breakfast?"
   "Yes, I have," replied the monk.
   "Then go wash your bowls."
   The monk heard that and got enlightenment.
   What did the monk attain?

—*Mu Mun Kwan*

W ITH CHANTING NOW OVER, it's time at last for
breakfast. Hungry after being up since what feels
like the middle of the night, I serve up a healthy por-
tion of rice and soybeans. There are only two condiments to
choose from: salt and peanut butter. Something tells me the jar
of peanut butter isn't going to last past the first few weeks. I
take a heaping spoonful of it and mix it into the rice and beans.
Though not normally my idea of an ideal breakfast, it tastes
surprisingly good.

Zen teaches, "Form is emptiness. Emptiness is form." This
means that everything is changing all the time. For example, a

tree grows for hundreds of years, changing shape, size, and color with every passing season. Eventually, it dies, is cut for firewood, is burned, and goes back into the earth, from which a new tree eventually grows again. So it isn't really a tree; it's a moving, changing phenomenon that we call "tree" for convenience sake.

The teaching continues: "Form is form. Emptiness is emptiness." This points to ordinary, everyday mind and is not attached to "emptiness." Things are just as they are. There it is in front of you. The tree is green.

What better way to learn about form and emptiness than by eating meditation?

A monk in our school named Mu Sang Sunim was once visiting the Centro Zen de Palma in Palma de Mallorca, Spain. It's no secret to those who know him that Mu Sang Sunim loves a nice piece of cake from time to time. His hosts, knowing he would enjoy coffee and cake, invited him out to a café one afternoon.

When the cake arrived, Mu Sang Sunim pointed to it, smiled a Cheshire-cat grin, and said to his hosts, "Form." Then he pointed to his stomach and said, "Emptiness."

They looked puzzled.

After polishing the cake off in a few bites, he pointed to the clean plate and said, "Emptiness." Then, pointing to his stomach, he said, "Form."

They all had a good laugh.

My bowl of rice and beans is empty now. I rinse it out with hot barley tea, rubbing the little bits of rice stuck to the bowl into the tea. Then I drink it all down with a big gulp.

Everything in the physical world comes and goes, yet something remains that is neither form nor emptiness. It is passed down for all people, for all time.

What is it?

Why *do* we eat every day?

When someone asked my teacher why he eats every day, he said, "I eat for you." The student didn't understand.

He said, "If I didn't eat, I couldn't teach you."

Only that.

8 Grace

> *Someone asked Joju, "Whence does the practitioner of the Way receive grace?"*
>
> *"Where do you not receive grace from?" answered Joju.*
>
> —*Radical Zen*

IT'S TIME TO GO OUTSIDE for work period. Bundled up in a heavy sweater and down vest, I put on my gloves, lace up my boots, and head out to cut wood. A friend has loaned me a rusty-looking metal bow saw. I've never used one before. Looking at its chipped orange handle, I realize I probably should have sprung for a new one.

There's about a quarter of a cord of wood already cut, stacked, and dried outside the cabin. There are several long trees on the ground in need of sawing, and a huge pile of logs to be split. It's gorgeous out. Huge evergreens everywhere. The sky's a brilliant blue. Winter in New England—you've got to love it.

I choose the smallest tree I can find, drag it to a sawhorse, and start sawing. Sawing, sawing, sawing . . . my arm is like a noodle after only a few minutes! The saw blade is dull. The deeper I cut, the more it gets stuck in the wood. With some dismay I realize this is going to take a lot longer than I thought. By the end of an hour and a half, the glorious "New England winter day" feeling has morphed into abject depression. I have cut only two logs. It occurs to me that I will either have to move more quickly during work period or burn less wood. I start to worry about rates of cutting and burning wood, and how long I can last out here without wood, but the mantra is there too, and for the moment it is stronger. It sends a quiet message that says everything has a way of working out, and not to spend another second speculating about how much wood it will take to last the winter. I smile inwardly, grateful for the true power in this practice. It's kicking in sooner than expected, better than any drug.

The next step is to get water. The well is about a quarter of a mile away, in a large clearing near a half-frozen pond, an outhouse, and two other cabins belonging to Joe and Terry Havens, the owners of this land. Both cabins are empty this winter.

The well, made of gray stones, is very deep. A bleached board with a crude handle covers the top. The pulley system on top looks pretty obvious, but there's a definite knack to how to toss the metal pail down so that it fills up just right. On the first attempt the pail lands upright, on top of the water. Peering over the edge down into the darkness, I see it floating there, empty.

"All right. So now, in addition to running out of wood, I won't be able to get water out of the well?"

The voices in my head are talking to me again, drowning out the mantra, which is now powerless in the face of their voluminous onslaught.

I imagine myself returning home early, tail between my legs, all because I couldn't get water out of the well.

Finally, after several more attempts, the bucket catches the water. It feels good and heavy and I pull it up, pouring its contents into the five-gallon jug from the front porch of my cabin. Victorious, I repeat this procedure until the jug is full to the top. Feeling a sense of accomplishment, I replace the cover on the well and, dusting off my gloves, think, "Another obstacle overcome!"

But the feeling of accomplishment is short-lived, indeed. Reaching down to lift the jug, I can hardly pick it up. Dismay sets in. I am on an emotional roller coaster, alternating every nanosecond between elation and misery.

"Surely all the other visitors here have been able to carry this big jug. Am I that much weaker than the rest of humanity?"

Huffing and puffing, I collapse on the porch of the cabin a quarter of a mile later, ready to call it a day.

It's 9:50 A.M.

Where has that mantra gone to?

Shim yo jung gu dae dharani . . .

When I decided to come out here and do this retreat, I was sure the biggest challenge would be the formal practice itself.

It never occurred to me that it would be such a physical fitness test just keeping warm or getting a drink of water.

Heat. Water.

How I've taken them for granted! Layman Pang once said, "My miraculous functioning is chopping wood and drawing water."

Now I understand.

9 Evening Practice

oh the evening wind hurries smoke our smoke
into the sky

—Zen Master Ikkyu, *Crow with No Mouth*

I T ' S N O W D I N N E R T I M E at the end of the day. The cheerful energy of broad daylight has given way to the pink and steel hues of twilight. I feel lonely. What am I doing here, in a forest, alone, in the prime of my youth? Shouldn't I be out dancing, at a party, having fun?

Someone advised me that having only two meals a day would be a good way to look at "attachment to food." Full of Zen ambition, I listened. To that end, I brought dried apricots, dates, figs, and prunes to go with evening tea. Exactly one hundred pieces, one for each night. Wrapped up in layers of long underwear, wearing a quilted gray patchwork robe borrowed from a monk, I sip the clear tea, eat this sweet, succulent date as slowly as possible, and suck on the pit. It was the biggest one in the bag. It disappears too fast.

There's stark, and then there's *stark*. This is *stark*. To counteract the bareness of the surroundings, I light every available kerosene lantern as well as several candles, resulting in a fairly bright cabin. After chanting I settle in for evening sitting, surrounded by the glowing, flickering light. Outside it is black and cold.

The fire is warm. The patchwork robe is warm. The birds have stopped singing. It is deafeningly still. The snow swallowed up all the sound into its white velvet blanket self.

I sit like a stone, mind and breath covered in the quiet snow. For two hours I lose myself in it.

10   A Diamond Sword

In your mind there is a diamond sword. If you want to
understand yourself, take it and cut off good and bad, long
and short, coming and going, high and low, God and Buddha.
Cut off all things.

—Zen Master Seung Sahn

VENING PRACTICE NOW OVER, I rinse my face
with warm water from a pot on top of the woodstove.
The towel smells smoky, which is kind of nice. Ahhhh
. . . here comes the best sound of the day: the unzipping of the
sleeping bag. I climb into its cozy womb, literally thrilled to lie
down after such a long and strenuous day. As I fall asleep, a
thought floats through my mind: "I did it!"

I survived the first day and all the practice forms of bowing,
sitting, chanting, walking, eating, and cutting wood. I carried
water from the well, surveyed the land a little bit. At times I
was convinced I made the right decision to come here. At other
times I seriously questioned my own sanity. Many kinds of minds

appeared and disappeared: sleepy mind, resistance mind, clear mind, fresh mind, bored mind, peaceful mind, fear mind, doubt mind, anger mind, desire mind, cold mind, hot mind, hungry mind, jealous mind, love mind, try mind. Beginner's mind. It was liberating to let them all come and go, rather than my usual pattern of getting caught up in the drama of each story—who said what, and where, and what to do about it.

And of course there was the squeaking of aching muscles, bones, and joints, like rusty hinges, not yet accustomed to such valiant Zen efforts.

Shim yo jung gu dae dharani . . . I'm about to drift off into an enlightened sleep. Things are going well.

Then there's the scratching.

What is that? My heart leaps into my mouth.

Adrenaline is a funny thing—it works instantly, without our having to think about it. My body is presently flooded with the stuff.

Scratch, scratch, scratch.

It's on my side of the cabin, near the bed! Now on the roof!

It must be a squirrel.

Is it?

I remember there's no lock on the door and no phone. This doesn't comfort me.

I play mind games with myself like this for a while. No one wins. Finally, one thought manages to prevail over the others. It says, over the loudspeaker of my brain, "You will never make it through a hundred days of this. Nor will you ever go beyond life and death if you can't learn how to deal with squirrels. Get a hold of yourself and do the mantra!"

This is my diamond sword, such as it is.

I don't care that it's more like a cheap metal knife. It will have to do for now.

Rolling Up Sleeves

11 A Seamless Monument

Emperor Su Tsung asked the National Teacher Hui Chung,
"After you die, what will you need?"
   The National Teacher said, "Build a seamless monument
for me."
   The Emperor said, "Please, Master, the monument's form?"
   The National Teacher was silent for a long time.
   Then he asked, "Do you understand?"

—*The Blue Cliff Record*

COULD END IT RIGHT HERE by saying, "This went on for the next ninety-nine days. The end."

The reason not to stop here, though, is this: if you keep practicing beyond one day, one month, or one year, your mind and heart become bigger and bigger. There is nothing new, really. We just keep revisiting the same lessons over and over until we digest them.

As we digest them, they become who we are.

It's powerful not to talk. It's been a few weeks now, and I don't miss it even slightly. People think that the silence is the most difficult aspect of a retreat only because they haven't tried it. The silence is the best part. It's unimaginably rich and spacious.

The sounds of the woods are varied and natural. The buzz in my head gives way over time to the cold creaking of branches, the soft slumping of snow melting off the roof, the chickadee's song. A silver pail as it hits the water in the well with a metallic splash. The rope on its rusty pulley as I pull it back up. The crunching of snow under my boots as I haul it back to the cabin. The wind has a thousand sounds. Sometimes it's a whisper, sometimes a high-pitched scream, sometimes faraway.

What a giant relief not to have to utter every thought, every observation, and every judgment that flits through my head. Letting things come and go, like the weather or like cars going by, takes all the weight out of them. Without any weight, there's nothing to hold on to.

Silence?

It's not silent at all! There's so much going on.

In the silence I can hear snow melting and it's beautiful.

12　A Finger Pointing to the Moon

Not dependent on words,
A special transmission outside the sutras,
Pointing directly to mind,
See your true nature, become Buddha.

—Zen Master Seung Sahn, *The Whole World Is a Single Flower*

AVING JUST RETURNED to the cabin after a late afternoon walk, I light a new fire and pour some tea. The day is winding down, not yet night. I'm getting used to it slowly, settling into the rhythm of the schedule. The pain in my thighs and knees from all the bowing is gone. I can cut wood and get water faster and more easily. Sometimes it's all pure and clear joy. Sometimes it's sad and lonely. It all comes and goes, like blue skies and clouds and wind. I try not to take it all personally, which helps enormously.

I open the *Blue Cliff Record* and read a Zen *kong-an* (also called a *koan*, a paradoxical question designed to transcend opposites). It grabs a hold of me right in the heart, touching the place deep inside that knows *I don't know anything.* Whenever someone else recognizes this point, even if it's just to say they don't know either, it's a great relief to me. It's as if they're saying, "You're not crazy. It really *is* empty."

Socrates used to walk around Athens and admonish his students, "Know thyself! Know thyself! Know thyself!"

One day, one of his students asked him, "Socrates, do you know yourself?"

"No, I don't," he replied, "but I understand this 'don't know.'"

The Zen tradition is famous for its thousands of kong-ans. A kong-an is a designed to give us the experience of not knowing. Here is one of the first kong-ans I ever heard.

At a talk at the Providence Zen Center, Dae Soen Sa Nim, holding a Zen stick in his hand, pointed to the cup he was drinking from and said to the audience, "Here is a cup. If you say it is a cup, you are attached to name and form and this stick will hit you thirty times. If you say it is not a cup, you are attached to emptiness and the stick will also hit you thirty times. What do you call it?"

The whole room woke up. Those of us in the audience began to unconsciously shift position, uncomfortable with not being able to answer. Since no one wanted to embarrass themselves in public by being wrong, no one even tried to answer. We sat there, a group of fifty or so, totally stuck.

Dae Soen Sa Nim then nudged the senior student to his left and said, "You show them," whereupon she just picked up the cup and drank from it. Smiles broke out at the simplicity of it.

Zen means demonstration, not explanation. In this case, it doesn't matter if it is a cup or not a cup, if it is form or emptiness, or if the teacher approves of you or doesn't approve of you. These are all opposites, which come from thinking. Zen transcends opposites and goes to the heart of what is useful: only quench your thirst. Just pick up the cup and drink. Even better still, offer a drink to the person who asked you the question so that person can taste for him- or herself.

When you are thirsty, no explanation in the world will quench your thirst like a glass of water. Similarly, when you embark on a spiritual journey, you have to taste it for yourself or it will never become yours. If it isn't yours, then it's never there when you really need it. Kong-an practice teaches us how to perceive our correct situation, correct relationship, and correct function and then respond accordingly.

The example of the cup kong-an is an easy, yet extremely useful one. Can I answer this one in everyday life when stuck in opposites like "Should I go live in this town or that one? Should I take this job or not? Am I right or am I wrong?" There are many thousands of kong-ans:

When you are born, where do you come from?
When you die, where do you go?
What is the purpose of your life?

This is why I'm here in these woods. Because even though technically I can "answer," I don't know.

13 Venturing into the Unknown

*outrageous eyes ears nose in the cold one silent tinkling bell
clear beautiful nudged by the wind hangs over the polished
railing*

—Zen Master Ikkyu, *Crow with No Mouth*

MID-FEBRUARY. Three fifteen A.M. the alarm goes off. I reach for the flashlight on the floor next to the bed and shine its light across the room to a thermos full of hot tea on the floor. It's so cold I can see my own breath, but I don't light the fire yet. After the first twenty or thirty bows my body will warm up. By the end of three hundred, I'll be down to a T-shirt and sweating. Outside the window is an impenetrable black darkness I'm as yet unaccustomed to.

This morning after bows, for whatever reason, perhaps being a little more comfortable in my new surroundings or just plain hot, I timidly open the door and peer out into the blackness, which at 3:50 looks an awful lot like *night*. No bears or bogeymen. I step tentatively onto the porch. The brisk air feels refreshing on sweaty skin. Looking up, there are a thousand stars glittering and blinking in the sky, like diamond earrings on the branches of the evergreens. As the boughs bend softly in the wind, I am drawn outside, as though there is a grand cosmic ball to which I have at last been invited. Nature is wearing her sequined coat. Everything is sparkling, stars above, snow below, in the moonlight.

An occasional dry creaking of the branches cracks through the silence.

Wow.

What in the world was I waiting for? I step off the porch and go for a short walk in the snow in the night. It is staggeringly beautiful! I am alone in the middle of the woods in the pitch dark and not afraid of a thing.

With each small venture into the unknown, I am rewarded with a new feeling: "I can do it!" It's very empowering. When you let go of your small self and bow to your true self, it's like saying to the world, "Please teach me. I am open to learning. I want to be with you."

Who would have ever thought that bowing, of all things, could teach you courage? When there is no separate, small self to protect and defend, then what's to be afraid of?

When you keep this mind, anything is possible.

14 Splitting Logs

There is nothing special about what I do each day;
I only keep myself in harmony with it.
Everywhere I neither accept nor reject anything.
Nowhere do I confirm or refute a thing.
Why do people say that red and purple differ?
There's no speck of dust on the blue mountain.
Supernatural powers and wonder-making works
Are but fetching water and the gathering of wood.

—Pang-Yun (Layman Pang), *Empty Cloud*

$\mathscr{E}$ACH MORNING looks slightly different in the small clearing behind the cabin, depending on whether it snowed the night before, or if the snow melted, or if the chipmunks came. Sometimes everything is glassed over in a sheet of ice. When the wind blows, the trees make a tinkling sound like delicate wind chimes. Sometimes it's slushy, cold, and gray. Other days, only piercing blue sky.

Splitting wood has become deeply satisfying. This must be because of the way you never know just exactly when the log will split in half. When it does, it's kind of thrilling. Each morning I look forward to work period as though it were recess at grammar school. After breakfast, with a belly full of hot rice and tea, I can't wait to put on my work clothes and head out back to chop wood. There's a neat pile of wood already split, stacked in a long row to my right. It's gratifying, to see all yesterday's work stacked there, with the wood supply growing bigger every day. The ground is snowy white, and in the center is the big splitting stump full of chops and ax slices from all the times I have swung and missed.

The ground around the stump is a ring of wood chips, pieces of bark, bits of dirt, hard berries, and pine needles. Though technically it's not beautiful, this picture of snow and stump and wood is somehow healing. My eyes haven't seen the hot pinks, neon greens, and bright oranges one finds in stores, on highway signs, computers, advertisements, and television, or in the world at large in a month. The only colors and shapes here are all nature's own. Up until only recently this view would have seemed a little boring to me—a bunch of wood chips on the ground in a quiet forest—but now that mind has settled down, things are beautiful just as they are. Buddha once said that being in nature is soothing to the human spirit. I'm finding it to be true.

I pick up a log and check the end to see if there might be a little crack in it already. If the log is really big, I hammer a wedge into it first, to leverage the cut. If it isn't too big around, I put it on its end and bring the ax directly down on that crack with my whole body. It doesn't usually split on the first try, but a good slice is made. On the second swing I aim for the same slice. After a few swings, suddenly it happens: the log splits in two. Inside are gorgeous deep channels of red and orange raw oak. Seeing the grain inside, I think about how long it took for that tree to grow, maybe a hundred years.

Mind is the same way. In an instant the truth can slice right through one of my tightly held illusions, just like that.

Picking up the next log, I feel a strong connection to everyone else who has ever cut wood, and to the people who still do to make their fires every day to cook and to stay warm. The past and the present come together as it splits in two.

I appreciate this chance to watch time and space disappear in the repetition and simplicity of something so ordinary as cutting wood.

15 The Chickadee Sermon

A bird in the hand is worth two in the bush.

—Proverb

I'M BOWING OUTSIDE on the porch after lunch. The thin smell of sandalwood incense curling into the open air conjures up a feeling of being in some ancient hermitage in Asia. Each time my knees hit the mat I see bleached, weathered boards the color of driftwood, with wide black cracks separating them. Each time I stand back up there's the sky, a blazing, fabulous blue. Green pine branches are bouncing gently in the wind.

Suddenly, from out of nowhere, a little black-and-white-striped chickadee heads straight for my face in a kamikaze dive, veering away just a centimeter before gouging my eyes out.

What's this? Here I am, living in harmony with nature, and the birds want to attack me?

Puzzled and disturbed, I return to the bows. Then the tiny dive-bomber comes at me again. For a brief moment I cock my head and wonder what's going on.

Then it dawns on me. Maybe she's *hungry!*

Excited, I grab a handful of sunflower seeds and hold it out toward the chickadee, who is poised on a nearby branch. That brave little bird flies straight over, lands on my hand, and curls her tiny, delicate claw around my finger precisely long enough to take one seed in her beak. She doesn't linger. As soon as she gets what she wants, she flits off to a nearby branch again. I rush back into the cabin for more seeds and try it again. Sure enough, my little friend comes back again for another.

Several other chickadees are watching this and want to participate. They approach like the first one, flitting from branch to branch, ever closer, weighing the risks and rewards in their minds. Some of them take the plunge, land on my finger, and take a seed. Others get very close and, at the last possible second, only an inch away from landing, they reconsider and veer off to a safe branch nearby.

Even among the chickadees, there are those who can make the leap of faith and those who can't. Perhaps it has something to do with how badly they want that seed. How many times in life do we want something, get close, and then back away at the last minute, afraid to take the risk? We humans are all like that. Most times our risks are small in comparison to the risk those birds took.

What are we afraid of? We are afraid of what people will think of us. We are afraid of losing our possessions. We are afraid to fail. Yet none of these are life-threatening, after all.

Sometimes we only care a little bit about waking up. When this is so, we spend the better part of a sitting period daydreaming. Other times we make a strong vow to wake up. At those times, we are like those little birds who take the plunge: vulnerable but brave, delicate and fearless at the same time.

We can experience and learn from both of these minds. One is not better than the other. Both are our teachers—like the old Zen saying, "Shouting into a valley: big shout, big echo; small shout, small echo."

16 Great Question, Great Faith, Great Courage

Great Question means, "I don't know if I can do this."
Great Faith means, "Yeah, but I'll try."
Great Courage means, "Only do it."

—Zen Master Su Bong

THE *mudra* in Zen is the way you hold your hands in your lap when you sit. The right hand is under the left, thumbs barely touching, as if you are holding an egg. If the thumbs fall apart, you are falling asleep. If they are turning white pressed against each other, you are trying too hard. Since I use a mala, moving one bead with every repetition of the mantra, it's easy to tell at the end of a sitting whether I have been clear or dreaming by seeing how many beads have been moved. Some days it seems to just "happen" and other days not. I don't want to try too hard, but if I don't try hard enough, I end up just sitting here and daydreaming. If I let my attention stray even for half a second, I'm gone again in a dream. Moment to moment I wrestle with this. To get it *just right*, not too hot, not too cold, not too loose, not too tight—this is why it's called "practice."

Buddha said right effort is one of the hardest things to achieve in practice. How much is "not enough" or "too much"? How to keep great faith, great courage, and great question alive without being a fanatic? How to become a great person, without having a "person" there who is "great"?

Animals do a better job at this than we humans. They seem to know just what to do and when. They know when it's going to rain. They know what kind of grass to eat when they get sick. They give birth without assistance. We humans can learn a lot from them, even Zen qualities like "great question," "great faith," and "great courage," if we would only take the time to observe how they behave. The truth of the whole universe, the great cosmos in its entirety, is right here in front of us in the call of a wild bird, in one breath, in the spider in the corner waiting for a fly.

There's a story about a cat who embodied this very quality of "great faith" we strive for as Zen students. She lived on a temple roof in Korea, where they have the most beautiful roofs in the world. Tiles—blue, burnt charcoal, slate gray, or terracotta—cover the buildings like patchwork monks' robes. In those tiles you can feel the chants and smell the incense of all the centuries of monks and nuns who have passed through. You can smell the Buddha and the tea and the rice wine in them.

You can see the sky and the clouds and the rain in them. And, most important, you can get miso and tofu that ferment in big pots that sit between the tiles.

Once when Dae Soen Sa Nim was a young monk staying at Hwa Gye Sah temple in Seoul, there was a scandal involving these pots on the roof. Every morning, the temple cook would go to the roof to get a few blocks of tofu for the traditional breakfast soup. One morning, he sensed that something was different. He counted the tofu blocks: there were only ninety-nine. There were supposed to be one hundred. Who would steal a block of tofu?

He thought it odd, but let it go, until he noticed it happened again the next morning, and the next. He reported this to the head monk, who called a meeting of all those living at the temple to ask if they knew anything about this. No one admitted it, so the abbot decided to post a guard on the roof each night to catch this scoundrel who would steal from the monastery. Every monk had to take a turn. One night during his watch, Dae Soen Sa Nim had nearly dozed off when he heard something . . .

Pad. Pad. Pad.

Quiet, quiet footsteps.

Without making a sound, Dae Soen Sa Nim trained his eyes on the pot of tofu, and there he saw the culprit: *a black cat!* Her eyes shone greenish yellow in the dark. She leapt silently up to the rim of the pot, parked herself there, and stared down into the depths. Like all cats, she wasn't fond of swimming and wasn't about to dive down to the bottom to get a block of tofu. But she wanted it, so she stared down at the water.

She had faith. She had courage. She had a question: Where is that tofu? Dae Soen Sa Nim watched, entranced. She was not attached to how long it would take, or if it would happen, or whether the tofu was high-quality or low-quality. She only did her job, putting all her cat forces to work, staring and staring, willing that tofu up to the surface, concentrating, until all of a sudden . . . *bloob, bloob, bloob!*

A single block rose from the depths to the top. She swiped it with her velvet paw and left without a trace.

This is how it should be done.

Practice means anything is possible.

17   Go Ask a Tree

On the bones of the Great Mountain
flowing water cleans the ancient Buddha's mind.
Do you understand the true meaning of this?
You must ask the pine tree.

—Zen Master Man Gong, from *The Whole World Is a Single Flower*

WHEN YOU SIT for a long time and don't speak, stuff comes out of the closet in your mind that you forgot was ever in there. Everything and everyone you ever knew or heard of comes to the surface, if only fleetingly. Old boyfriends. Sandwiches you ate on the beach, and how the beach looked and smelled. Your parents, and brothers and sisters. Cars you've driven. Books you've read. Friends. Mountains. Poems. Funerals. Weddings. Babies. Game-show prizes. As Vipassana teacher Jack Kornfield used to say at retreats, "It's all in there. Everything your second-grade teacher ever said to you, every movie and commercial—it's all there." Some people and places come back more often than others. These are usually the people and places you either love the most or have some unresolved conflict with.

Afternoon. Sitting. Sunlight plays with form, making dancing shadows on the walls and floor of the cabin. It's windy outside, but warm in the cabin. Long-underwear warm. Robe warm. Mind is sticky in the molasses, so dreams come. Thoughts come. Images come, in 3-D Technicolor. The person who keeps popping up is my close friend and teacher Zen Master Su Bong, who died, too young, in his early fifties. He was the one I met back at that first long retreat in Barre, Massachusetts, with Zen Master Seung Sahn, when they came to speak to our group. Su Bong was a big inspiration for me. He's always in the back of my mind, like a Buddha I was lucky enough to know personally.

Su Bong Sunim was smart in some ways, yet really stupid in several other ways. This made him a great Zen student and teacher. (It is said that to penetrate the true meaning of Zen you must be "completely stupid" and throw away all your ideas and preconceived notions about life. But you also need an equal dose of intelligence to recognize that this "stupid" mind is actually very wise.) Su Bong fancied himself an ancient seeker, and in many ways he was. Half Korean and half Chinese by descent, he had almond brown eyes, a huge warm smile, and beautiful hands. He grew up in Hawaii and loved all things Asian: Zen, noodles, rice cakes, calligraphy, and kung-fu movies, which I think he may have seen too many of.

For example, early on in his practice, he was invited out to dinner in Los Angeles with a group of dignitaries from Japan who were visiting a Zen master named Kozan Roshi. This invitation was a great honor for Su Bong Sunim, who promptly went out and bought himself what he thought would be an appropriate outfit to meet such exotic Zen folk: a set of baby blue Chinese pajama-like loungewear and a pair of black Tai chi shoes. Looking and feeling every bit the part of a true mystic, he showed up in an elegant restaurant in modern-day L.A. in this attire to meet the foreign guests. When he arrived, there they were, all in Armani suits, staring at him in disdain as if he were some sort of nut case. No doubt with his active imagination he had probably envisioned them carrying scrolls and wearing embroidered gowns, seated around the table discussing haiku between sips of green tea. Su Bong told me he never felt so silly in his life, in his baby blue pajamas with nowhere to hide.

This is what I mean by smart and stupid. He was smart enough to have embraced the wisdom he encountered in his meetings with Zen masters and to have chosen that as a direction in life, yet stupid enough to think he was living in a kung-fu movie and to wear the baby blue pajamas to dinner. This is what I liked best about him. Even now, as I sit here on my cushion, this image of him in pale blue silk floats across my mind, and I can't suppress a burst of giddy laughter.

Once Su Bong Sunim, in response to an answer Zen Master Seung Sahn had given at a public talk, raised his hand and said, "I don't believe you."

"Wonderful!" replied Seung Sahn. "That's correct. Don't believe me. Don't believe Buddha. Don't believe anybody. If you want to know what you are, go ask a tree."

So, every night after his work as a carpenter, Su Bong would come home, take a shower, drag his mat and cushion to the backyard, and park himself in front of a big maple tree.

"Tree," he would ask, "what am I?"

No answer.

This went on for a long time.

Inspired by the thought of my friend and teacher, I go outside and ask the tree, "What am I?"

If you want to know what the tree answered, go outside and try it yourself.

18 Ten Dumb Years

ten dumb years I wanted things to be different furious proud I
still feel it
one summer midnight in my little boat on Lake Biwa
caaaawweeeee
father when I was a boy you left us now I forgive you

—Zen Master Ikkyu, *Crow with No Mouth*

JUST AT THE END of work period a light snow begins to
fall. Walking back to the cabin, carrying water from the
well, under those soft-falling white crystals, I'm invigor-
ated, having split many logs today. Stamping off the snow on
the steps of the porch, I take off my big work boots, gloves, and
vest and sit by the stove to warm up for a moment. I pour a cup
of hot roasted barley tea, warming my fingers on the ceramic
cup. As I sip on it, it warms my insides and reminds me of a
conversation I had once with Su Bong Sunim.

There's a famous Zen teaching that goes, "Sipping green
tea, I stop the war." When I read it for the first time, I thought,
"Wow! That's really good." So the next time I went for a formal

kong-an interview with Su Bong Sunim, I mentioned it to him. His response was, "No good."

Stunned, I asked, "Why?"

He said, "When you drink tea, just drink tea. Leave off the part about 'I stop the war.' That part is bullshit, okay?"

Feeling grateful to have been around a such keen-eyed teacher, without warning I suddenly think of war. How *do* you stop war? Images flood my head of people killing each other, blood flowing, limbs blown off. Bodies lying limp like rag dolls, in fatigues or civilian clothes. Always someone's child. Someone's father. Someone's lover.

The grief I compressed and hid away when my father died in Vietnam suddenly rushes out from its hiding place. Surely the eighth wonder of the world must be memory. What is its physical location, its chemistry, and its process? How is it that we can vividly remember the tip of something, as if it were from another lifetime, only to have it vanish just as quickly back into the recesses of wherever it resides? Maybe it isn't stored after all, but rather activated by a related experience, appearing only when that particular surface gets scratched. I don't know. What is interesting is how the reflection of our past experiences can sleep for years at a time and then, triggered, come rushing out with all the ferocity of Niagara Falls, nearly knocking us over unawares.

My dad died of natural causes in Saigon when I was six years old. He had been stationed there as an air-force officer for nine months prior to his death. When he flew home in a coffin, all his promises to my mom and brother and sister and me about the fun we would have together when he came home were instantly and forever broken in a thousand splintery shards. I don't think about it as I go through each day of life. I don't remember him even slightly as I enter into conversations with people, make lunch, or walk down the street. But every now and then the pain of losing him so young in life floods through my veins afresh, stinging and burning as if it were yesterday. Tears spill out in an instant. I am blubbering, chin quivering, with my heart aching suddenly and out of nowhere. Or maybe I see a news clip of troops coming home from some international incident. The soldiers get off the plane in their crisp, clean uniforms and start running across the tarmac. Their wives and children jump into their arms, and everyone is crying with happiness. That one really gets me. I so wish it could have been our family there, with that happy ending. Then the news clip is over. Dad disappears again, sometimes for a long time.

Where did he go?

I could sit here in this cabin in the woods for fifty years, a hundred years, ten thousand years.

don't know
don't know
always and everywhere
only don't know

19   Cognition Is Not the Path

Mind is not Buddha.
Cognition is not the path.

—Zen Master Nam Cheon

WEDNESDAY. Early morning. Stars become snow and cover the ground in a white blanket.

The sky is white. The ground is white. Insulated. Silent. White. Branches bow low under the weight of it. So perfect.

All without thinking.

How is it possible that we have to try so hard to be simple? It's funny, really. Going through all of this just to be my natural self. Zen homework isn't like any other homework. There's no reading, no studying, and no report card. The less thinking you have, the better Zen student you are. Just put your whole self into each and every thing you do until it becomes part of you

and you become part of it. Like it is outside today, with no visible demarcation between up or down, heaven or earth.

Mind is not Buddha.

Cognition is not the path.

All that's left is white.

20 Bath Day

*In olden times there were sixteen Bodhisattvas. When it was
time for the monks to wash, the Bodhisattvas filed in to bathe.
Suddenly, they attained the basis of water.*
   All of you Zen worthies, how will you understand?

—*The Blue Cliff Record*

BATH DAY IS TODAY. On this most special day, I make
multiple trips to the well and haul ten or fifteen extra
gallons of water back to the cabin for the high point in
sensual pleasure for the week. It's quite an operation to prepare
it all. I love every bit of it, because the reward of feeling the hot
water run all over my skin is well worth the work.

In order to prepare the bath, I get a blasting good fire going
in the woodstove. All the collected water is in jugs on the floor,
ready to be heated up. There are two "burners" on top of the
stove, which are actually just two black iron lids with handles
on them that can be moved away to reveal holes directly over
the flames. The big black pot is on the back burner and a

speckled, glazed enamel pitcher on the front. I bring both of them to a full boil and set up the "tub."

The tub is a beige plastic basin just big enough to sit my butt in. There's a smaller purple pail in front of that for my feet. A towel is on a chair, and my dirty clothes from the past six days are in a pile next to it. The inside of the cabin is nice and warm because of the huge fire. Once the water comes to the boiling point, I partially fill the beige and purple basins on the floor, then add some cold water until the temperature is just right. I take off my clothes and stand naked in the cabin. Since coming here, my body has been covered at all times, wrapped up in layers of thermal underwear, socks, and warm clothes. Without all those heavy clothes on, I feel extra naked. For once in my life I am lean and strong. It feels good to have the fat off, to know that every muscle is being used for something good.

I sit down in the hot water in the beige basin and, bringing my knees up to my chest, immerse my feet in the purple pail. Next to me is the big enamel pitcher full of water, which I now pour over my head. It runs down my chest and back, and I instantly attain a state of mind much higher than nirvana. I lather up and get sudsy all over and pour more water down my legs and arms for a second time. This is by far the most sensually fantastic experience of the week. I feel the warm water like never before, deeply appreciating the comfort and pleasure that come from the way it feels on my skin.

After lolling about in this heavenly realm for a good half hour or so, scrubbing and rinsing and refilling, I step out and fill the basins with my dirty clothes, letting them soak in the bathwater. Still wet, I scrub the socks and underwear and thermals one by one with a bar of soap. No need to worry that someone will see me naked at the door dumping out dirty bathwater into the snow—there's no one here! Now I fill the basins with hot clean water from the stove top and let the clothes soak a second time as I towel off, brush my hair, and put on some clean clothes. I rinse and wring everything out a third time and hang it to dry from the ceiling rafters and around the stove. I must be out of my mind—alone in a cabin with wet thermal underwear and socks hanging from everywhere, dripping, but I love it!

Once on Diamond Mountain in Korea, a monk went to the hot springs on his way to the Zen center at the top. After a steamy herbal bath in which he scrubbed himself clean, he thanked the owner. "Your hot tub is the best in all Korea!"

"Oh, wonderful," she said. "Your face looks very clean. May I ask you a question?"

"Of course! I am a Diamond Sutra master, okay? Ask me *anything!*" replied the monk.

"Okay, here is my question, Great Master. Today you cleaned your body in the hot tub. How do you clean your mind?"

The monk was stuck, turning five shades of red and white from embarrassment.

"*You!* You say you are a Diamond Sutra *master?* You don't even understand its most essential meaning—how can you go around and try to teach others?" said the woman.

If you have a mind, clean it.

If you have no mind, dry off and go to evening practice.

Hard Training

21   Sun-Face Buddha, Moon-Face Buddha

Mind is not Buddha.
Cognition is not the Path.

—Zen Master Nam Cheon, *Mu Mun Kwan*

I T ' S E A R LY M A R C H . The days and weeks are passing quickly now. For some strange reason I'm sick today, lying on the bed in a fetal position just to keep from throwing up. My head is splitting, my stomach nauseated. The miso must have gone bad.

I find myself wondering, "Two months alone in the woods. What did I attain?"

Attain.

This is a very dangerous word for a Zen student. One of the first things we are told when we start practicing is that we must "attain" the Buddha's mind, yet in the next breath the teacher will say, "If you want to attain something, you already missed the point."

No matter who we are, we want to attain something. We want to go beyond merely *understanding* life and death. We think that to "attain" is to get rid of everything in the way of attainment. If we could get just get rid of the nasty little impediments of wanting, holding, desire, fear, anger, and ignorance, then nothing would be in the way and we would attain enlightenment. We think that attainment is a state we have to get to, a destination, like Los Angeles or Boston. Through hard training, lots of concentration, and sincere effort, we'll arrive. Once there, this other pesky stuff won't bother us anymore.

Lying here now, sick as a dog, I don't feel as though I have attained anything at all outside of simply being here and experiencing all the ups and downs, the clarity and the confusion, and the fear and the peace that have all come and gone. It occurs to me in this vulnerable state that regardless of the practice, the teachings, or what I attain or don't attain, I can't control this body. It will get sick, grow old, and die whether I like it or not, whether I am enlightened or not, and, most especially, whether I am ready or not. I guess I've always half assumed that someone was there in the background to protect me from this truth—God, Buddha, family, teachers, close friends. Today it hits me hard that *there is no safety net.* No one in the world can do this work for me. No one else can help me.

Even God and Buddha can't save me.

I have to do it myself.

This is it: hard training. We've all heard about the "hard training" in Zen. Those classic photographs of Japanese monks walking barefoot in the snow are what we think of first. The bottom line, though, what hard training *really* means, is that every idea we have ever had or ever will have ultimately betrays us. Hard training has nothing to do with how many bows you do, how many days you fast, or how many kong-ans you pass. It means there is no point of reference, no place to stay, no lasting thing, no eyes, no ears, no nose, no tongue, no body, and no mind. Zen Master Dok Sahn put it this way after his enlightenment: "Even though one masters profound philosophies, it is like placing a single strand of hair in the great sky. Even if one gains all the essential knowledge in the world, it is like throwing a drop of water into a deep ravine."

There isn't anything anyone can give us, hard or easy—which is precisely what makes it hard.

How to come so close to the bone you are the bone?

How to stay like this?

How to let go of that when you can't, and just move on to the next thing, never looking back?

For ten thousand years.

22   Waiting for a Sweet One

One day Mullah Nasrudin was sitting in the market in front of a
big basket of red hot chili peppers. With tears streaming down his
cheeks, eyes bloodshot, face red, and nose running, he kept eating
one after another. Every now and then he let out a big howl they
were so hot!

  One of his students approached him and asked, "Mullah!
What on earth are you doing? Why do you keep eating them?"

  "I'm waiting for a sweet one," he replied.

—Idries Shaw, *The Incomparable Mullah Nasrudin*

THIS AFTERNOON, sitting feels interminably long.
One would think that after two solid months of nothing
but uninterrupted Zen practice I would be able to control my mind at will, but no such luck. Try as I might, I cannot
focus on the mantra at all. I'm sick of it. I want something with
taste to it, not the cold clear water of clarity. How about a story
line and a happy ending? Girl is released from spiritual quest.
Girl finds true love. Girl sips margarita on white sandy beach.
Girl lives happily ever after.

How many trillions of times replaying the same dreams? My whole life I've been engaged in one continuous visual and auditory hallucination. I catch bits of conversation with people I don't know, about topics I don't care about. And I sit, riveted, like someone surfing the channels on TV all day and night, watching other people's lives, games, and dramas—*for what?* It doesn't seem to matter if it's a good dream or a bad dream. I chase them all just the same, like Mullah Nasrudin, sitting in the market eating those burning-hot chili peppers. If leaving everyone and everything I know behind and coming out here doesn't do the trick, what *will* stop this crazy habit?

Zen Master Bankei said we human beings retain all the things we see and hear, and at certain times these things are reflected back to us in precise detail. As long as we don't involve ourselves with them and just let them be, they can't help but stop. Then it's the same as if they never arose in the first place.

Right?

Will the day ever come when I will have had enough of it?

Deep in a cave, water drips on a stone, over years and years, and centuries and eons. Finally, a hole is made. Through the hole comes light and wind and the ability to see through to the other side.

Just the fact that the hole can be made at all gives me faith.

That's my sweet pepper!

23   You Decide

Thus it is said:
The path into the light seems dark,
the path forward seems to go back,
the direct path seems long,
true power seems weak,
true purity seems tarnished,
true steadfastness seems changeable,
true clarity seems obscure,
the greatest art seems unsophisticated,
the greatest love seems indifferent,
the greatest wisdom seems childish.
The Tao is nowhere to be found.
Yet it nourishes and completes all things.

—*Tao Te Ching*, translated by Stephen Mitchell

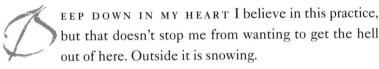EEP DOWN IN MY HEART I believe in this practice, but that doesn't stop me from wanting to get the hell out of here. Outside it is snowing.

Again.

I long for spring, for life, for anything else but this. Today this tiny cabin is bleaker than bleak. Bare floorboards, dirt in the cracks between them, the sink that isn't hooked up to plumbing of any kind, the cold ashes in a metal bucket next to the woodstove—what am I doing here? Wouldn't it be so much easier to just leave? I could pack up my stuff, walk the three miles to the phone booth down the road, call a cab, and get out of here by this afternoon. It would be quite easy actually—what's to stop me? I'm ready to jump out of my skin for no apparent reason, like a horse kicking the stall, not that there's anyplace else to gallop off to.

Instead, I head for one of the few clearings in these woods, craving space, craving light. This world of nothing but frozen earth and leaves is boring and dry and dead. I swear to myself if I ever do one of these retreats again it will be in a place with fewer trees and more light. I remind myself not to daydream about that now—I am already here on *this* retreat, in *this* moment. Then, like Buddha talking to me, I hear Dae Soen Sa Nim's voice in the back of my mind whispering those awful words he loves to say:

"I can," then you can.
"I cannot," then you cannot.
You decide.

Moment by moment the choice is there: to surrender to infinite possibility or to lock myself inside the walls of pessimism, limitation, and subjectivity. I exhale slowly several times, remembering a story my friend Mu Sang Sunim told me.

Once, when Mu Sang Sunim was feeling very down, he went and asked Dae Soen Sa Nim what to do.

Dae Soen Sa Nim said, "Do one hundred and eight bows."

"I feel too bad to bow," said Mu Sang Sunim.

"Then go sit."

"I can't sit," said Mu Sang Sunim.

"Then go down to the river, look straight at it, and shout *Kwan Seum Bosal*," said Dae Soen Sa Nim.

"Okay," said Mu Sang Sunim, who went and did it and felt much better.

I go outside my cabin and chant *Kwan Seum Bosal*.

It works!

I *can*, even when I think I can't.

After all, this is the real power of it.

24 Un Mun's "Cake"

Someone asked Un Mun, "What is the speech that goes beyond
Buddhas and patriarchs?"
Un Mun said, "Cake."

—*The Blue Cliff Record*

M Y EARLIER ASSUMPTION that the peanut butter
would be gone after a few weeks was dead-on correct. Weeks ago I licked that jar so clean even an ant
wouldn't have found a meal there. There were also one hundred pieces of fruit—one for each night. They're all gone too,
even though there are still seven weeks to go. It's eye-opening
to experience the depth of my need for food and how it super-
sedes all the other needs I have always considered crucial to my
happiness. Coming from a privileged economic class, I've taken
the basic gifts of survival for granted, never appreciating just
how big a role they play in my life.

I have always wanted to try fasting for a short period and decide this is as good a time as any since the only two foods I'll

have to give up are rice and beans. I'm sick of them both anyway. Fasting is legendary in many spiritual traditions. Zen Master Seung Sahn fasted for his entire one-hundred-day solo retreat when he was young. He ate only crushed pine-needle powder.

For three and a half months.

His body turned green from it. When he returned to the temple, they gave him acupuncture treatments and burned *moxa* (a spongy herb used in acupuncture) on his belly for months afterwards to get his skin color back to normal. I will opt for a more modest regimen: three weeks of tea and miso broth.

I am not trying to be macho. I am genuinely curious about the nature of desire. My whole life has been spent chasing one desire after another. Where does it come from and how does it control me? What happens if I don't follow each desire that comes into my mind? What happens if I don't eat for a short period?

What happens is what any idiot could have guessed would happen: I am ravenously hungry. The rice and beans I was so sick of before would taste like exotic delicacies to me now. There's no way to get around this feeling of hunger. No way to avoid the pangs in my stomach and the intense desire for a taste of bread, of butter, of *something*. I make many cups of miso broth and tea each day. My mind is focused almost exclusively on food-related topics. I alternate between the mantra and visions of lasagna, pumpkin pie, and chocolate honey-dipped crullers. I write a few imaginary cookbooks and open an imaginary Zen restaurant called Café Joju.

What happened to all those other desires? Love, enlightenment, adventure, fame . . . all leveled to nothing. All extraneous. I only want food. Food on my tongue, taste in my mouth. I don't care what taste it is.

Food is life.

Why am I alive?

What is this life for?

What will I do with it?

Shim yo jung gu dae dharani . . . The mantra is singing itself, coursing through my whole body. It feels as though I've reached some higher state of being, until I get hungry again. On day nineteen, with just two days to go, my hands, all by themselves, reach into the big brown bag of rice, measure out a cup, and dump it into the pot. I say to myself, "No, no! Don't do it! Only two days left. Just drink some tea," but it's no use. I add water to the uncooked rice in the pot and light the fire even as I chastise myself not to. The smell of it cooking is intoxicating, full, precious. I'm salivating like a dog.

I learned something about desire on this fast.

Desire is very, very powerful.

But you know what? Even stronger than that is the taste of this rice!

I'll keep trying.

25   Who's There?

If I go to the Hell filled with swords,
Swords will break into pieces by themselves.
If I go to the Hell filled with boiling metal,
Boiling metal will dry itself up.
If I go to the Hell of endless suffering,
The Hell will be destroyed of itself.
If I go to the world of warlike demons,
Demons will surrender themselves.
Karma has no self-nature; it arises from the mind.
If mind disappears, karma disappears.
If you keep the clear mind of a Bodhisattva
No difficulty will arise.
Buddha's fortune will always be with you.

—From *The Ten Thousand Eyes and Hands Sutra*

MIDNIGHT. I have some extra energy and am outside doing bows on the porch. It's glorious out, moonlight shining everywhere, illuminating the snow and the trees. The mantra is going strong, when out of nowhere I hear the distinct crunching of footsteps and voices coming toward my cabin.

"Who's there?" I wonder.

Who the *hell* is that? I freeze, ears straining to hear. Is it my imagination again? Is it just a chipmunk? No, most definitely not. There are muffled voices. One is a man, for sure. I can't tell how many people are there. I immediately remember every scary movie I have ever seen. *In Cold Blood,* where they came and killed the whole family for no reason at all. Sick stories from the newspaper about rape and murder flash through my mind. Someone must have found out I'm up here all alone. They're coming for me, I know it. My body is frozen. Knees like jelly. I can't go back inside the cabin with no locks on the door. I'd be trapped in there, unable to keep them out. I have no car to run to, no phone, nobody to scream to for help. Who would hear me? The mantra is out the window. All the practice may as well have been in vain because I am utterly scared shitless. I could grab the ax—wait, what if they're stronger than I am and they use it to hack me up? I better not grab the ax. Maybe I should hide the ax. I don't want to get cut up with an ax. That would not be good. No, no.

Crunch, crunch, crunch. The footsteps are getting closer. The voices are getting louder. Who in the name of God would be coming up here in the middle of the night? For what reason, other than to do me in? I take a silent step toward the edge of the porch, ears nearly straining themselves off the sides of my head. I'm careful not to make a sound as I inch my way off the porch toward the only means of escape—the woods.

The snow is hard and crunchy. They'll hear me as I try to run. I'm frozen in a half crouch on the ground, listening.

Wait, what's this? One of the voices sounds like that of a woman. She's laughing. It's a group of a few people. They are just talking. They don't sound evil. They're just walking, and laughing, and getting closer.

A wave of relief floods through my body as I realize who it must be: it's the Havens family! They own this property and have another cabin not far from here. They must have returned from California earlier than expected! Ha! Ha!

I'm saved.

Sure enough, the footsteps pass by and the voices are friendly. It's Joe and Terry Havens. I can't see them, but I know it must be them.

If I were completely at one with the universe, there would be nothing to be afraid of, not even death. As clear as I may fancy myself to be, when there's turbulence on the plane my heart goes into my mouth. If the phone rings in the middle of the night, I'm jolted out of my sleep, sure someone just died. And if I'm alone in the woods and hear footsteps near my cabin at one in the morning, after weeks of seeing no one out here, it's time for a coronary.

I know there's nothing to be delivered from, but I want deliverance anyway. I want to be living, walking, and breathing in the shining light of universal truth at all times and never know fear again. Never, ever. Not only that, I want everyone else in the world to have this too. I must be nuts.

My knees are shaking so badly I have to sit down for a minute. It takes a few long minutes to still my beating heart. A little bit of humble pie. I'm no Buddha, beyond life and death. I'm Jane from Rhode Island, and I've just been granted a stay of execution.

26 A Water Buffalo Passing Through a Window

Oh Jo said, "It's like a water buffalo passing through a window. His head, horns, body . . . everything has all passed through. Why is it that his tail cannot?"

—*Mu Mun Kwan*

TODAY I WOKE UP hopeful that the sun would break through. Again my hopes are dashed. It's even grayer and gloomier than the day before. How can it possibly continue snowing so much? It's early April already. I desperately need to get out of this tiny cabin. For two solid weeks it has snowed heavily every day. The snow is now so deep it requires snowshoes to get to the well. I can't even get outside for work period to cut wood. The chopping stump on the ground is buried under a foot of snow.

As if exiled in Siberia, I find myself swearing in between mantras. Okay, this *sucks*. Gone are the happy revelations of the chickadee eating out of my hand. I don't care about finding out about my true self or anything else. I only want one thing: the sun. After all this meditation I can still be angry at . . . *the sky???* I am hopeless, let's face it. If ever I had a deep moment before, I'm as shallow as they come now.

This whole "living close to nature" paradigm is for the birds. Given the choice of having electricity, only a complete idiot would prefer cutting wood and gathering twigs all day to make her own fire. Turn on the lights, did you say? Oh, no thanks. I'd much rather clean five soot-covered kerosene-lantern globes with old crinkled newspaper every morning because they are black from the night before. Draw a bath? Nonsense! I prefer cutting down the trees, splitting the logs, making a fire, boiling the water, and then sitting in a plastic basin just barely big enough to get my rear end in.

Sometimes it's so incredibly difficult to be here, I wonder why I came at all. Dae Soen Sa Nim always says, "Don't make 'difficult,' don't make 'easy.' If you make difficult, then difficult! If you make easy, then very easy!"

If you don't make *anything,* then what?

The moment you don't make anything, Buddha's "right effort" is achieved. Right effort is no effort. To get to the place of doing things effortlessly takes a hell of a lot of effort. I suck it up one more time, exhale a retinue of complaining, angry Buddhas back out to the universe, and return to the mantra.

Maybe the sun will come out tomorrow.

27 Fake Dream Craziness

why is it all so beautiful this fake dream
this craziness why?

—Zen Master Ikkyu, *Crow with No Mouth*

THE JUDGE CAME by during sitting today.

Wait, what am I saying? The Judge *lives here* with me, incessantly commenting on everything, from how I look to whether she thinks the last thought that came by was a good one or a bad one.

My little Judge!

After all, I've never been without her—except perhaps as an infant, but that was too long ago to remember. The Judge feels it is her mission to make comparisons. She does her job extremely well.

First and foremost, she compares me to everyone else. Depending on her mood and who she compares me to, I am either a superhero or a selfish pig.

"You're great!" she tells me, full of conviction.

I feel fabulous for a moment.

"I take it back—you're not so great. In fact, you're an idiot. You just fell for me again."

I concur with her. I am the dumbest Zen slob on earth, just another self-righteous, ego-ridden, pathetic little sentient being.

Second, the Judge compares all things to each other even though it makes no sense. For example, she might say, "This life is very strange" (as someone once said, "Compared to what?").

Or she might exclaim, "Oh, this kind of snow is *much* better than that kind of snow." She simply never lets up, which is quite extraordinary when you stop to consider how much work it is.

The Judge doesn't stop there. She then moves on to judge herself as well as the judgments she continually makes. Judging judgments—now there's a good one. It's like a hall of mirrors. Following her whims makes me weary. I wish the Judge would take a little vacation—doesn't she ever get tired of it? Or need a break? I've suggested this to her, but she insists she is passionate about her work.

I've decided now, after listening to her all morning, to just let her do her job. I'll do mine, which is to go straight ahead with the mantra and not pay one scrap of attention to her. I'll let her be like the wind blowing by. Let her go ahead and scream; she's just the call of a wild bird to me. Or an airplane flying overhead. Why should I be like a dog that runs after every bone she likes to throw?

She comes out of nowhere and she returns to nowhere, just like everything else.

I bow three times to her.

Now that I think about it, she's actually one of the best teachers I ever had.

Thank you for your teaching, Judge.

28 Un Mun's Utmost Master

A monk asked Un Mun, "What is the utmost master?"
"This utmost master is a lump of shit."

—Zen Master Un Mum

B ECAUSE THE BASIC essentials of living close to nature require so much of my personal involvement, I'm paying more attention to details like water and trash. It's time to empty the chamber pot on the front porch that is full to the brim with the dung of yours truly. During work period I decide to take it down to the outhouse to empty it. It is surprisingly heavy. The deep snow doesn't make for easy walking. Trying not to break through the thin ice crust on the top layer of snow, I make my way to the outhouse, a small distance away. Every couple of steps my boot breaks through, and I sink all the way up to my knees.

Should have worn snowshoes.

I finally get there, huffing and puffing, and put the pot down to rest a minute. This is the only visible waste I have generated in the past few weeks. At home I can fill two trash barrels with tons of junk every week, but out here there's just this small recyclable bucket. I take off the lid and turn the bucket upside down. It's frozen solid as a rock. No problem, I think. I'll just get a big stick and poke it out. I break four hefty sticks on that pile of frozen shit. After fifteen minutes of assaulting it with all my might, it occurs to me that an easier way to get it out would be to melt it. I lug it all the way back to the cabin so I can be there in time for cleanup and bows at 9:45.

Between 11:00 and 1:00 there's a sunny spot in the small clearing next to the cabin. For the next few days I bring the pot out during walking meditation, take the lid off, and place it in the center of the only patch of sunshine there is. As the sun moves, I move the pot too, hoping to melt at least the top layer. Even though it melts a little bit while the sun is out, it freezes over again quickly. This is turning into a bona fide dilemma. I don't have any other containers to use.

This little project is actually kind of humorous. Here I am, ostensibly seeking that which is beyond life and death, moving a pot full of my own poop three inches to the right every half an hour so it will melt. To complicate matters, some days there is no sun and it's snowing heavily.

Three days later the sun comes out and it's a warm day. Finally. After lunch I decide to check on the melting project. I open the lid to add a fresh contribution and what do I see? A little gray mouse snuggling up and rolling around in the melted top layer of my shit. His whiskers covered in brown, he is reveling in it. A day at the spa for him. He looks up at me. Our eyes meet for a split second. Then I let out the biggest scream you've ever heard, dropping the lid with a clang on the porch as he runs for his life. My heart is banging like a pile driver, this being the biggest excitement and most eye contact I've had with any other being thus far on the retreat. I am at least able to empty the top level of the bucket, thanks to the warmer temperatures.

To see another creature nuzzling around in what I would consider the most disgusting place on earth is quite a shock. In this universe, everything is eating something else. One man's ceiling is another man's floor, so to speak. And all of it is going around and around—from me and you to the mouse, to the bug, back into the earth, fertilizing the next fruit or vegetable, back to you and me. Around and around we go.

Pretty good system.

That little mouse and I become friends. The next day, when I lift the lid to add more poop, there he is again, enjoying himself like a child playing in the mud. I look at him, add my fresh contribution to his survival, and quietly close the lid and go away.

Two thousand years ago, Zen Master Un Mun, when asked about the utmost master, said, "This utmost master is a lump of shit."

I now know what he means.

29 The Willow Is Green, the Flowers Are Red

When you hear the wooden chicken crow
You will understand the country where your mind was born.
Outside my window in the garden
The willow is green, the flower is red.

—Zen Master Ma Jo

T HE PAST FEW DAYS, probably just from being silent and doing a mantra for so long, everything has jumped into a kind of magic "ultrastate." The substance of the universe glimmers in shining lines through the snow, swims up the grooves in the bark of the trees, and bounces off the branches into a trillion points of light.

My feet aren't my feet. The ground below is coming out of my head. All my teeth are dancing in my jaw, as if no longer attached to the bone. The backs of my knees can hear. Branches near and far are clouds and skin and air and earth. For a few days everything is in this "heightened" reality. It is fantastic, completely unencumbered by concepts of any kind.

Then, like silver mercury, it slips through my fingers and is gone.

Try as I might to hit upon some strategy that is guaranteed to always work, it never happens. How do I get myself to remember to let go of everything *all the time?*

What about all the times I forget to do that?

We cannot predict what will appear in our lives at any given moment. Sometimes when it's dark outside, the wind screeches and howls, and there is only an overwhelming feeling of impermanence everywhere. I see my body as a corpse—nothing more than a sack of flesh, bones, blood, pus, urine, and excrement. After all, that's what it is, isn't it? The image scares me, as I think about the fact that one day I will die and someone will put my body in a coffin. This keeps me up half the night practicing hard.

The next morning, sunlight comes streaming through the window. The dark night has passed. It seems like years ago that my heart beat in such terror. All my cares are limited to preparing the rice for breakfast. There's no life-threatening urgency to practice hard. There is just a relaxing into things.

This life of ours is surely like a Ferris wheel. Around and around it goes, with a life of its own. When you get off, with both feet on the ground, look out the window at the garden. One thing is clear.

Green willow.

Red flower.

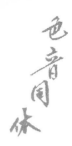

30 A Lotus Grows in the Mud

it takes horseshit to grow bamboo
and it too longs forever weeps begs to the wind

—Zen Master Ikkyu, *Crow with No Mouth*

WANT." "I have." "I need." "I, I, I." It's endless! If something beautiful comes out of all this suffering and passion, may it save all beings because it sure as hell isn't saving me.

Today I am so dying for something other than rice and beans to eat. If I even so much as *look at* another soybean, I am going to throw up. I refuse to ever eat one again. Ever.

I am presently visualizing coffee from Dunkin' Donuts, in one of those fantastic cardboard cups with the soothing pink and orange logo on it. Right now, if you put that in front of me beside the most handsome Hollywood actor, I would definitely choose the Dunkin' Donuts coffee. No contest.

I see croissant sandwiches. During sitting I plan my future as a caterer and design menus from appetizers to desserts for fictitious weddings and birthday parties. I keep trying to get back to the breath and the mantra, but the catering scenarios are coming back with a vengeance. After a lunch of the usual rice and sunflower seeds, I head out for a walk. It's sunny out, almost springlike. Early afternoon, with this kind of gorgeous weather, the only thing missing really *is* the food.

About a mile down the dirt road, between several pine trees, I see a most unusual sight: a parked car. The orange color doesn't fit in with everything else. I don't know whose it is, but its presence can only mean one thing: *there might be something to eat in that car!*

Could it be? An open window!

As if in a Yogi Bear cartoon, I spy an actual *picnic basket* in the backseat on the floor. Yes, a bona fide old-fashioned picnic basket, with the checkered cloth, the little wicker handles, and the whole bit.

Lust mind kicks in. I look to my left, then to my right, making sure no other animal can catch my prey. The thought flits across my mind that I shouldn't reach in that window or in that picnic basket, but it is instantly overpowered by the feeling of the wicker handle against the palm of my quivering little hand. Lifting the lid, I find my deepest prayer has been answered: Lorna Doones!!! How many can I take without the owner noticing an errant Zen student has been here? Perhaps it is a gift from God for all this hard training. Or is it a test of will?

I don't care. Grabbing four cookies, I jam one into my mouth, reserving the others for later. All clarity is gone. The mantra is gone. My body has been taken over by a group of aliens. I hurry back to the cabin propelled by an extreme adrenaline rush and try to savor the other three. Ten seconds of pleasure and then, tragically, they are gone. I could go back and get more, but it's two miles round-trip and dark now. Plus I'd break the schedule and I can't do that . . . can I? No, I can't.

Guilty now, I'm out of balance.

"I've strayed."

"I'm no good."

"It doesn't matter."

"Yes, it does! Dae Soen Sa Nim ate only pine needles! He would never have fallen for the Lorna Doones!"

"Jesus Christ, Jane, you chose, for better or worse, to adhere to a regimen most people would never have undertaken in a million years. Why not allow yourself this small transgression?"

"Will the owners of the car notice the cookies are missing?"

"Why have I lost my mind, like a crazy fool, for a fleeting taste of cookies?"

"What's so powerful about taste anyway?"

"On the other hand, in the grand scheme of things, what's a few Lorna Doones? Why obsess over such an insignificant thing?"

Mind can make a mountain out of a molehill, regardless of the content. Like a pebble in a pond, the ripples of each thought go outward in circles farther than you can imagine. It's humbling to know that on a normal day in my usual life back home, this level of mind activity is going on—times ten million. It's just that it's going so fast that I can't notice it.

There is no sutra that can illustrate the mud of endless desire mind as well as those cookies did.

Bamboo will grow here, and lotus flowers.

Spring Comes

31 For You

Zen Master Seung Sahn once asked a student, "Why are you sitting for the winter?"

"Because I want to."

"That's a number-one bad answer! You ask me the same question, okay?"

"Okay. Why are you sitting for the winter?"

"For you."

THE MANTRA this morning is a bare wisp of a filament, quiet, steady, and porous enough to allow in fast-moving shadows on the floor, flickering and changing with the clouds passing and the wind. Branches, leaves, and the side of my head rush to and fro in silhouette. A plane flies overhead through it all, through me, through the mantra, through the shadows of the branches. This has all been going on for thousands of years, yet it is only now.

No one is in any of it.

You've no doubt heard the expression "Nobody home." This is usually used in a derogatory fashion, indicating that the person in question is less than brilliant. We Buddhists have found another way to look at "Nobody home."

"Nobody home" means that no matter how much you reduce yourself, down to the cellular level, the electrons, the quarks, whatever the smallest part is you can reference, it is moving and changing. There is not one thing in this whole wide world that is fixed. If you find it, it's already gone. Since there isn't one single solitary thing in the whole universe that is fixed, it stands to reason there is no constant "self" that is experiencing any of this. Any reasonable person can understand this—it actually makes common sense.

As basic as this notion may be, it is the ever elusive essence of the Buddhist path. This is the point we keep harping on, we keep trying to realize, and we keep coming back to over and over again. Why does it require so much time and energy? Because our habit of approaching the world from "my" point of view is so deeply embedded in us that it's difficult to remember that the *my* part is just smoke and mirrors. All the problems and confusion we've ever had are based in this misperception that whatever is happening, it's happening to "me." Everything. Anger, desire, fear, jealousy, hurt—all of it. Every time we take a closer look, we can see there is no such thing.

Dae Soen Sa Nim has penetrated this phenomenon by changing his habit of looking at life from the point of view of "I" to having no point of view at all. Since he has no point of view, his mind is like the universe: vast, wide, and limitless.

This is how he can say such an outrageous thing like "For you." And really mean it.

The fact that he means it and lives it every day inspires me so much.

I tell myself over and over, "If he can do it, I can do it."

This is the kind of ambition the world could use more of.

32 Sangha

Someone once asked Zen Master Man Gong, "What is the most precious thing in Buddhism?"
"Sangha," he answered.

RINGING THE EVENING BELL at 7:00 P.M. before chanting, I think about how at just this moment there are many thousands of people around the world doing the exact same thing I'm doing. At Providence Zen Center's Diamond Hill Monastery, for example, there are thirty or forty people sitting the winter retreat, Kyol Che, for ninety days. Someone is just now ringing the evening bell too, their hand picking up a mallet in Rhode Island just as mine is picking up one here. In Warsaw Zen Center they are doing the same thing, except it's a six-hour time difference. In Korea, at Hwa Gye Sah, Su Dok Sah, Joeng Hye Sah, and at hundreds of temples big and small, there are monks and nuns doing the same thing, except it's a twelve-hour time difference.

Then of course there are the Tibetan Buddhists, and the Vipassana practitioners, and all the thousands of people in Japan and China and India and Thailand and Burma and Vietnam and Cambodia and many other countries. Add to that all the people practicing at home, and there is no moment on earth when someone isn't practicing somewhere. Add to that all the other spiritual traditions and religions of the world and I'd say we have a critical mass of human beings who are helping to make the world a better place.

You can't leave out those who aren't interested, for they too are part of the sangha. The moon and the stars and all animals and insects and flowers and trees are the sangha. The air and the sun and the water are the sangha.

All things and all beings are included.

This is why Zen Master Man Gong said, "Sangha."

33 Nature's Genius

nobody knows I'm a storm I'm
dawn on the mountain twilight on the town

—Zen Master Ikkyu, *Crow with No Mouth*

AT 4:00 EACH AFTERNOON I take a walk. This is one of my favorite parts of the schedule. Standing up and stretching out stiff legs after the long afternoon sitting session, I put on my jacket and head up the mountain. The well-trodden path of snow from the cabin is covered with a canopy of evergreens. Thin needles are scattered here and there on the snow, just so, better than any landscape artist could ever design. Some days the light from the sky is purple-gray, other days it's rose and gold. Each kind of light creates a different feeling and casts a different hue on the rock, the ice, and the laurel bushes, which are plentiful on this land. Once I am on the path, the cool, moist air sweeps over me, washing my mind and body clean of thought worlds that don't exist. Green tunnels of bowed branches beckon me into their healing never-never land world.

Seeing a fallen tree, I stop and notice all the activity on this "dead" log. There's moss all over it, and lichen. Under the rotting bark is the most fertile dirt. Soon there will be a world of activity in here. Small green shoots will grow out of the center of the log and turn into big trees one day.

I head past the clearing by the well, and past the Havenses' empty cabin. Just past that is an old low-lying mineral-spring hut, surrounded by big gray stones. A hundred years ago this place, Temenos, was a healing resort because of its mineral springs. I climb down on the stones and listen to the water bubbling. There are a few melted candles on the rocks down here. I bet it's a nice place to cool off on a hot summer day.

Just past the mineral-spring hut is the trail that leads to the top of the mountain. Along the way are birch groves, narrow icy slopes of rock, and shiny green thickets of laurel poking out through the ever present snow. Picking up a smooth gray stone, I wonder how old it is. How many elements does it contain? Einstein said its energy is its mass times the speed of light squared. Then are we the same or different? I throw it as far as I can off the top of the mountain.

Thinking: different.

No thinking: no difference.

Nature is the real genius of us all.

If we can be as quiet as the stone, as flowing as the river, as big as the sky, and fertile as the earth, like nature, we can be geniuses too.

34   Peace Isn't Luck

peace isn't luck for six years stand facing a silent wall
until the you of your face melts like a candle

—Zen Master Ikkyu, *Crow with No Mouth*

A SHAFT OF GOLD LIGHT streams across my field of vision as I stare at the yellow pinewood floor this afternoon. Specks of dust are illuminated, whirling and sparkling, dancing. The chickadee's song goes into my scalp and down the back of my spine like liquid notes turned into heat. The sun is warming one side of my face.

I am so at peace. There's nothing more to need or want. Nowhere I'd rather be. The humming of my mind is at rest, like sediment that has settled to the bottom of a glass of water. It's still, perfect. There's a warm, deep, calm feeling permeating everywhere.

How could I have missed this pleasure for so many years?

35   Wild Fox Spirit

A monk asked Tae Kwang, "Jang Gyeong said, 'Joyful praise
at a ceremonial meal'—what is the true meaning?"
Tae Kwang did a dance.
The monk bowed.
Tae Kwang asked, "What have you seen, that you bow?"
The monk did a dance.
Tae Kwang said, "You wild fox spirit!"

—The Blue Cliff Record

IN THIS AUSTERE SETTING it's funny I could feel such a deep happiness. This kind of pure joy is the profound contentment of appreciating life and every small experience it brings. It's the satisfaction of having really put yourself into something one hundred percent. How often in life do we really do that?

People often think Zen is a cold and unforgiving practice. I too used to think that the "self" is a big block of karma to be "gotten through," and thus was inclined to put my head down into the wind on a retreat like this, as if there were some mountain of ego-rock to be gotten over. This kind of practice only begets more misery. Though there are difficulties and hard times along the way, the general approach to practice can also be one of exploration, motivated by a genuine question and curiosity about life and one's place in it.

If you love what you do, you'll want to do more of it.

Tonight it rained. The sound of it pelting crazily on the roof, while I am dry inside, makes me happy. After it dissipates, I get up to go outside and get a whiff of fresh air. As I open the door to the porch, my heart stops. The whole world is dripping, peacefully. How could I possibly be lucky enough to witness this? I write the following after coming back in to practice:

Dark night.
The rain just stopped.
Standing on the porch
With a cup of tea . . .
Dripping near
Dripping far
Earth smell
Oh God.

This is unbelievable. I feel like my friend Billy, who plays guitar in a rockabilly band in Boston. He loves to play the guitar so much that during the breaks he comes off the stage, drops to the ground on his kneepad-clad knees, sweat streaming down his face, and exclaims incredulously to whoever will listen, "I get *paid* to do this!"

No one is paying me to be out here, but I feel like Billy does. I am getting paid in a way. Paid in happiness. Paid with the sounds of dripping water. Paid with the smell of earth and pine. Paid with peace and feeling comfortable in my own skin. Paid with a reason to live.

A long time ago, when I saw the picture of Suzuki Roshi on the back cover of *Zen Mind, Beginner's Mind*, I saw the peace in his eyes. After some years of practice I feel a little like that too.

It's only going to get better with time.

36 Rapture

People say that what we're all seeking is a meaning for life. . . .
I think what we're really seeking is an experience of being alive, so
that our life experiences on the purely physical plane will have
resonance within our innermost being and reality, so that we can
actually feel the rapture of being alive.

—Joseph Campbell

ONE OF THE MAIN PURPOSES of my coming here was to get my mind and body in the same place at the same time. More than three months into this adventure, it's happening more frequently—certainly more so than when I first arrived. By making my focus smaller and smaller, everything is getting bigger and bigger. Just rinsing out the breakfast dishes, I am happy. There's a vast space around things in which anything is possible. A sense of rapture permeates even the smallest activities of the day.

This word "rapture" is not one we are accustomed to using because it typically is reserved for the most rarefied of moments of pleasure like great sex or a gorgeous beach or a wonderful piece of music. Why not let that kind of joy into all the "little" things, like smelling the air, hearing the insects singing on a spring evening, washing the dishes, or seeing our family at the end of a day's work? Isn't that what our whole life is?

Joy comes from appreciation. Appreciation comes from paying attention. Paying attention is the practice of Zen. It's so simple, yet look how I have had to strip away everything, come out here to a cabin in the middle of nowhere, adhere to an unforgiving schedule, and stick it out through all the ups and downs in order to discover it.

It's very humbling.

At the same time, it's inspiring, because it means I don't have to wait for rapture to come at only the "rarefied" moments. It's possible to change my habit from dreaming to waking up. Then this rapturous joy will enter my life more regularly. What's going on "outside" will match the "inside." I won't just be going through the motions of living—I'll actually be alive.

Having the mind and the body in the same place at the same time solves about ninety-nine percent of the matter.

The other one percent, of course, is what you do with it.

37 Sink into This World

So much suffering in Nirvana castles
So joyous to sink into this world.

When in old clothes you call yourself Buddha,
What do you call yourself in silk?

Wooden man went out with shoes at night,
Stone woman came back with hat in morning.

You, for the first time, can perceive when you
Pick up the moon three times as it floats on the pond.

—Zen Master Seung Sahn, *Bone of Space*

EVEN THOUGH THE FLOWERS aren't here yet, spring has come. Barely visible, the tiniest of buds are growing from the smooth branches of the trees, emerging, gestational. Bugs are mating everywhere—on the sides of trees, on tops of leaves, underneath the leaves, by the pond, on the woodpile. Walking back to the cabin from the well, I look at my watch. There's still half an hour before the break is over. Along the way, a flash of lime green catches my eye and I stop to take a closer look. The snow has melted away, exposing patches of verdant moss. Is it because it's been so cold and frozen for so long that the mere sight of green moss makes me giddy? Or is it because everything has become so simple that each small thing is so wonderful? I lie down on it, all velvet, fresh, and green, and gaze up at the sky through a canopy of green pine branches and fast-moving clouds.

There is wisdom in the way the ancients set up a typical monastic year. Three months of practice in the winter are followed by three months of freedom in the spring. Three months of practice in the summer are followed by three months of freedom in the fall. In Korea, the long winter retreat like this one is called Kyol Che, meaning "tight dharma." The period following Kyol Che is called *Hae Jae*, meaning "loose dharma." Like a guitar that needs constant tuning to make a good song, we humans need tune-ups as well. Living too tight for too long a time produces a tight person. Living too loose produces a loose person.

A person in perfect tune requires periods of both.

Now, it's almost spring. The hard, icy edges of winter are melting and something inside me is melting too. I am softening, blooming, and opening. Taking off layers of clothing, I can move my limbs more freely. Stretching, inhaling, coming alive. Melting into spring. It's time for flowers to bloom and for all the little creatures to be born.

What will all this hard Zen practice give birth to?

The seasons point to the true way, without words, entering through our pores and becoming part of us, as we are part of them.

Spring comes.

Flowers blooming everywhere.

38 Very Soft Is True Strength

Very soft is true strength.
With harmony comes luck.
Goodness brings you virtue.
Follow situation, then get happiness.
Forbearance will make you a great person.

—Zen Master Seung Sahn

B Y NOW I GUESS you could say I'm in shape Zen-wise. I could probably win a marathon if it involved bowing, and I could definitely sit longer without moving than most people. I'm lean in body and mind—a Zen athlete in contention for an Olympic Zen medal. I used to think strength in Zen was all discipline, toughness, and willpower, but now I can really appreciate the other half of that equation: knowing how to yield, receive, listen, and surrender. Keeping an open mind and heart in all situations. Letting go of everything and giving your whole life to all beings. This is the real marrow of it.

Zen Master Seung Sahn breaks my heart. Not in a mushy way—he'd never let me get away with that. He breaks my heart because he is so consistently *right*, which only comes from years of hard training, clear seeing, and right motivation.

He told me, "Follow situation, then get happiness." The situation on this retreat has been the schedule and the practice. I followed it. Got happiness. It hasn't been easy; nor has it been exactly fun. Yet, perhaps because of the very difficulty of it and continuing through it anyway, something wonderful has emerged, like returning to what's originally true and right. If I keep doing this, it can only bring more of the same.

In one of my favorite Zen books, *Dropping Ashes on the Buddha*, there's a wonderful story about this point. A Zen Master named To An was disguised as a wandering monk. As he came to a small town, he met another monk who began to talk about his master. "Every day he does one thousand prostrations. He eats only once a day. He hasn't left the temple for almost thirty years. He is always sitting Zen. He is the greatest Zen master in all of China."

To An said, "Well, he sounds like an extraordinary man. I can't do any of these things. I can't bow a thousand times a day, but my mind is never lazy. I can't eat only once a day, but I never desire food. I can't stay in a temple for more than a short time, but wherever I go I have no hindrance. I can't sit Zen for very long, but I never give rise to thinking."

The monk told his teacher of this, who came running out to find To An. Deeply touched, he realizes that To An's practice was not only for himself, but for everyone.

There it is again: "Not for me."

It's for all beings.

Sinking, sinking, sinking in.
Down into my bones and heart.
I'm not a perfect Bodhisattva.
I have a long way to go, but it's all right.
I'm going.

39 Everything Just Like This Is Buddha

All of us together must let go of our "I." We must put it all down.
Only when we return to our before-thinking mind is it possible to
eliminate the confrontation, hostility, fighting, and killing that are
destroying this world. If your mind becomes clear like space, then
everything you see and hear will be the truth. Mountain is blue,
water is flowing. The dog barks, "Woof, woof!" Salt is salty,
sugar is sweet.

When we see that the world is one with our true self, then we
attain "correct life," which means attaining our correct situation,
relationship, and function. This is called "world peace."

This is Zen.

—Zen Master Seung Sahn

ONE OF MY FAVORITE teaching phrases of Dae Soen
Sa Nim's is "Everything just like *this* is Buddha." It
originally came from a line in a poem by Master Pai
Chang. It's a simple way of saying that what we are doing now
is already *it.*

Buddha is not somewhere else. If you are walking down the
road, looking at the trees, that is Buddha. If the sound of the

geese honking above fills your head, that is Buddha. If you are making rice, that is Buddha. If you are tired and angry, that is Buddha too. You have to remember only this and you will always be complete.

Soon I will return to the "marketplace." I look forward to it, yet not without the proper amount of respect. It's easy to remember "Everything just like this is Buddha" living alone, in silence, with no bills to pay and no one else to think about.

How to manage that going sixty-five miles an hour with the radio on?

This chance to live with the wind in the pines for one hundred glorious days and nights, to watch the interplay of form and light without interruption, to find happiness in the taste of barley tea, and to feel at home with myself just the way I am— it was hard won, and no doubt it will be hard to come by in the future.

Every day we breathe fresh air. We see brilliant colors and smell a thousand smells. We hear the sounds of nature: rain, wind, birds singing, branches creaking, leaves blowing, thunder, dawn. We hear the sounds of humanity, the din of traffic, a train's whistle, children playing in the afternoon. We think somehow it will always be ours for the taking, but we must keep in mind that each experience we have is very precious.

It is said that each moment of life is a chance that only comes along once every five hundred years. We must live our lives accordingly, with every fiber of respect and attention we can muster.

We will not have the chance to do it again.

40   Returning Home

Once, at the end of a ninety-day meditation retreat, a student asked Zen Master Seung Sahn, "After all this hard training, adhering to a tight schedule, we are free to do anything we want. Now what shall we do?"

Dae Soen Sa Nim, eyes bright, answered gleefully, "Go sightseeing!"

ONE HUNDRED DAYS. Where did they go? I light the last fire this morning. Make the last tea. For once in my life, I am in no hurry to get to the "next thing."

I scrubbed the cabin clean yesterday to pay respects to all it has given me and to leave it in spotless condition for whoever comes next. The stove is empty of its old ashes. Fresh, dry kindling and a few logs are placed beside it. The glass globes on the kerosene lanterns are clean. My smoky-smelling clothes, ax, saw, flashlight, gloves, and a few Zen books, all faithful companions, have been packed away.

It looks perfect. These golden pine floorboards are more beautiful in their simplicity than any marble floors or velvet carpets money could buy. I know every crack, every whorl, and every grain in them like the back of my hand. The sliding glass door behind the altar is crystal clear, revealing the gorgeous woods. New yellow candles saved for the occasion have been placed in silver candlesticks.

To think that in a few short hours, someone will be coming to pick me up, well, it's kind of thrilling. I'll see all the people I love. I will have access to anything I want to eat. Running water. A hot bath. Clean clothes. But my overwhelming emotion is sadness. All too soon the machinations of the world and its demands to speak, produce, declare, pay, do, and act will take their toll upon the simple person standing here this morning. In no time flat, I'll be running around, going to work, going to the movies, getting stressed out, and talking all day long about sheer nonsense.

I could almost cry, but the practice won't let me.

I will miss the incense curling around the Buddha's head in the afternoon light, the silver birches, the mountain laurels, and all the smells and sounds of nature. I will miss making fires and living simply, the silence and the peace of it all. Thanks to all of it, thanks to Buddha, thanks to my teachers, both living and dead.

I promise to never, ever lose this pure mind.

I promise to continue for ten thousand years.

The bright red of a car appears outside the window.

The engine sputters off. Keys are jingling.

My friend is walking toward the cabin.

It's time to go home.

Epilogue

Since completing this retreat many years ago, I have continued practicing with Zen Master Seung Sahn and now have begun to teach others interested in learning Zen. One can only wonder, after an intense experience like a hundred-day retreat, Does the practice actually work when you are back home, living with your family and going to work every day?

The answer is a resounding yes. But, as you may have suspected, there's a catch: you have to continue practicing. Over the years, the initially noticeable demarcation between formal practice and everyday life gradually disappears. You realize that each and every thing you do is an opportunity to wake up, to learn, to open your heart and mind. If Zen were limited to only sitting on a small black cushion on a little blue mat, then it wouldn't really be worth all the effort we put into it.

The lessons we learn while doing formal practice about our human emotions—desire, anger, ignorance, fear, resistance, and grasping, as well as generosity, love, wisdom, courage, and compassion—are all learned on the cushion, so that when a situation arises in our everyday lives with a spouse, a neighbor, a co-worker, or even a stranger, our eyes will see clearly. Our ears will hear clearly. Our true self will function perfectly, just the way it does when we are alone in the woods.

There are now six billion people living on the planet, and the number is growing exponentially larger every day. Most of these six billion people are attached to their idea of "my" life, "my" country, "my" way, "my" religion, "my" possessions—and so the world is full of suffering and fighting. Each one of us is a part of this problem, and each one of us is the solution.

There's a wonderful bumper sticker from the 1970s that says, "Think global. Act local." This is good Zen teaching. Acting locally means finding your true self and letting it function correctly in this moment. Thinking globally means living your life for all beings.

The true way is always right in front of you.

Appendix:
The Great Dharani

shin-myo jang-gu dae-da-ra-ni
na-mo-ra da-na da-ra ya-ya
na-mak ar-ya ba-ro-gi-je sae-ba-ra-ya
mo-ji sa-da-ba-ya
ma-ha sa-da-ba-ya
ma-ha ga-ro-ni-ga-ya

om sal-ba-ba-ye su da-ra-na
ga-ra-ya da-sa-myong
na-mak-ka-ri-da-ba
i-mam ar-ya ba-ro-gi-je
sae-ba-ra da-ba i-ra-gan-ta
na-mak ha-ri-na-ya ma-bal-ta
i-sa-mi sal-bal-ta sa-da-nam
su-ban a-ye-yom sal-ba bo-da-nam
ba-ba-mar-a nii-su-da-gam da-nya-ta

om a-ro-gye a-ro-ga
ma-ji-ro-ga ji-ga-ran-je
hye-hye-ha-rye ma-ha mo-ji sa-da-ba
sa-ma-ra sa-ma-ra ha-ri-na-ya
gu-ro-gu-ro gal-ma sa-da-ya sa-da-ya

do-ro-do-ro mi-yon-je
ma-ha mi-yon-je da-ra da-ra
da-rin na-rye sae-ba-ra ja-ra-ja-ra
ma-ra-mi-ma-ra a-ma-ra
mol-che-ye hye-hye ro-gye sae-ba-ra
ra-a mi-sa-mi na-sa-ya
na-bye sa-mi sa-mi na-sa-ya

mo-ha ja-ra mi-sa-mi
na-sa-ya ho-ro-ho-ro ma-ra-ho-ro
ha-rye ba na-ma-na-ba
sa-ra sa-ra shi-ri shi-ri
so-ro so-ro mot-cha mot-cha
mo-da-ya mo-da-ya
mae-da-ri-ya ni-ra-gan-ta
ga-ma-sa nal-sa-nam
ba-ra-ha-ra-na-ya

ma-nak-sa-ba-ha
shit-ta-ya sa-ba-ha
ma-ha-shit-ta-ya sa-ba-ha
shit-ta-yu-ye sae-ba-ra-ya sa-ba-ha
ni-ra-gan-ta-ya sa-ba-ha
ba-ra-ha mok-ka shing-ha
mok-ka-ya sa-ba-ha

ba-na-ma ha-ta-ya sa-ba-ha
ja-ga-ra yok-ta-ya sa-ba-ha
sang-ka som-na-nye mo-da-na-ya sa-ba-ha
ma-ha-ra gu-ta da-ra-ya sa-ba-ha

ba-ma-sa gan-ta i-sa-shi che-da
ga-rin-na i-na-ya sa-ba-ha

mya-ga-ra jal-ma ni-ba
sa-na-ya sa-ba-ha na-mo-ra
da-na-da-ra ya-ya na-mak ar-ya
ba-ro gi-je sae-ba-ra-ya
sa-ba-ha

Acknowledgments

First and foremost, thank you to Zen Master Seung Sahn for bringing Zen to life in such a direct and skillful way that it is nothing short of contagious. The way he lives his life every day is the gold standard of what a human being is capable of.

Thanks to all of the teachers and students of the Kwan Um School of Zen throughout the world, most especially to the late Zen Master Su Bong, whose teaching and friendship will remain forever close to my heart. Thanks to the Venerable Geshe Tsultrim Gyelsten for countless hours of patient instruction, to Joseph Goldstein, Jack Kornfield, Sunanda, the late Bhante Seevali, and all the teachers of the Insight Meditation Society in Barre, Massachusetts, for clear and excellent teaching. Thanks to the late Joe and Teresina Havens, and to all those who support Temenos, for making retreat cabins available for sojourners of every tradition.

Thanks to the Venerable Mu Sang Sunim, Zen Master Wu Kwang, Zen Master Bon Haeng, Dyan Eagles, Trudy Goodman, Bridget Duff, Heather Moulton, Bill Deacon, and Ralph Woodward for providing great editorial advice and moral support along the way. Thanks to Zen Master Seung Sahn for the use of his calligraphy throughout the book. Thanks to Stephen Berg for his brilliant translations of Zen Master Ikkyu in *Crow with No Mouth*, and to Yoel Hoffman for his equally wonderful collection of Zen Master Joju's teachings in his book entitled *Radical Zen*. Finally, thanks to Stephen Mitchell for compiling the teachings of Zen Master Seung Sahn in *Dropping Ashes on the Buddha*. These three books have helped me in so many ways and are all core holdings for any serious Zen student's library.

Special thanks to Currie McLaughlin, Angel Kyodo Williams, James Najarian, J. W. Harrington, Gail McMeekin, and Ashton Applewhite, who helped this first-time writer navigate the art of bringing a book to publication. Thanks to my literary agent, Eileen Cope, who believed in this book based on a phone call from a stranger—her encouragement was largely responsible for its coming to fruition. Thanks to my editors at Harper-Collins, Gideon Weil, Liz Perle, Anne Connolly, Lisa Zuniga, and Kathy Reigstad, whose meticulous and generous advice was invaluable.

Thanks to Loretta and Larry Anderson and Katarzyna Dobisz for watching Olivia so I could write. To my husband, Piotrek Dobisz, thank you for the enormous time and effort you contributed on every level, and for all your love, support, and Zen advice.

And lastly, to my beautiful daughter, Olivia Rose, this is for you, and for all children. May you grow up in a world filled with love and peace.

Bibliography

Bankei Zen. Translations from the Record of Bankei by Peter Haskel. Edited by Yoshito Hakeda. New York: Grove Weidenfeld, 1984.

The Blue Cliff Record. Translated by Zen Master Seung Sahn. Providence, RI: Kwan Um School of Zen, 1983.

Bone of Space: Zen Poems by Zen Master Seung Sahn. San Francisco: Four Seasons Foundation, 1982.

Dropping Ashes on the Buddha: The Teaching of Zen Master Seung Sahn. Compiled and edited by Stephen Mitchell. New York: Grove Weidenfeld, 1976.

Empty Cloud: The Autobiography of the Chinese Zen Master Xu Yun. Translated by Charles Yuk. Longmead, Shaftesbury, Dorset: Element Books, 1988.

Zen Master Ikkyu. *Crow with No Mouth.* Translated by Stephen Berg. Port Townsend, WA: Copper Canyon Press, 1989.

The Mu Mun Kwan. Translated by Zen Master Seung Sahn. Providence, RI: Kwan Um School of Zen, 1983.

One Robe, One Bowl: The Zen Poetry of Ryokan. Translated and introduced by John Stevens. New York and Tokyo: Weatherhill.

Radical Zen: The Sayings of Joshu. Translated with a Commentary by Yoel Hoffman. Brookline, MA: Autumn Press, 1978.

Shah, Idries. *The Exploits of the Incomparable Mulla Nasrudin.* London: Octagon Press, 1983.

The View from Cold Mountain: Poems of Han Shan and Shih-Te. Translated by Arthur Tobias, James Sanford, and J. P. Seaton. Edited by Dennis Mahoney. Buffalo, NY: White Pine Press, 1982.

Zen Master Seung Sahn. *The Whole World Is a Single Flower: 365 Kong-ans for Everyday Life.* Boston, MA: Charles E. Tuttle, 1992. (Reprint as *Zen: The Perfect Companion.* New York: Black Dog & Leventhal Publishers, 2003.)

About the Author

Jane Dobisz (Zen Master Bon Yeon) is the Guiding Teacher of the Cambridge Zen Center in Massachusetts. She has practiced in various traditions of Buddhism for twenty-five years. Jane has led several ninety-day intensive retreats (in the United States, Europe, and South Africa) attended by hundreds of students from around the world. She is the editor of "The Whole World Is a Single Flower" by Zen Master Seung Sahn. Jane lives in the Boston area with her husband and daughter. For more information on her teaching schedule please visit www.thewisdomofsolitude.com.